Reiki

AND THE SEVEN CHAKRAS

Reiki

AND THE SEVEN CHAKRAS

your essential guide

Richard Ellis

Vermilion
LONDON

10

First published in 2002 by Vermilion,
an imprint of Ebury Press, Random House,
20 Vauxhall Bridge Road, London SW1V 2SA
www.randomhouse.co.uk

Addresses for companies within The Random House Group can be found at
www.rbooks.co.uk

The Random House Group Limited Reg. No. 954009

A CIP catalogue record for this book is available from the British Library.

The Random House Group Limited supports The Forest Stewardship Council (FSC),
the leading international forest certification organisation. All our titles that are printed
on Greenpeace approved FSC certified paper carry the FSC logo.
Our paper procurement policy can be found at www.rbooks.co.uk/environment

Printed and bound in the UK by CPI Mackays, Chatham ME5 8TD

ISBN 9780091882907

For Maya

Acknowledgements

I would like to thank firstly my mother Sue and father Peter for their love and moral support not only whilst writing this book, but throughout my whole life. I Love you so much.

Magda for her love, shoulder massages, enthusiasm and her research into chakra exercises. Also for selflessly looking after our daughter for six weeks alone whilst I worked non-stop to complete this project.

My daughter Maya and my niece Poppy for bringing me so much joy, keeping me in my heart and reminding me of what is important.

My sister Debbie and her partner Andy for their great generosity and a wonderful week in the Canadian lakes which gave me great inspiration.

Paul Young for his vision and artistry which made this book look so Now!

Caroline Ness for editing my ramblings and bringing her own personal understanding and wisdom to my book.

Lesley McOwan and Lovelock & Co for their professional expertise in producing and designing this book.

My friend, agent and fellow Reiki master David Parrish without whom none of this would have ever happened. Thank you for your understanding, insight, feedback, patience, integrity and love.

Lawrence Ellyard for his personal research into Dr Usui's life story and for generously letting me include this material in the chapter 'A Modern History'.

My Reiki master June Woods for teaching me to let it flow.

Debra & Greg Cass for being living examples to follow.

My dear friends, Jen, Toni and Fi for being in my life.

Those who have trusted me as a holder of healing space.

Anyone who has helped me on my way that I have forgotten, thank you.

Contents

Preface:
The Book's Intention

Over the last seven years of working closely with energy, it is my experience that the key to understanding the healing process on all levels lies in a greater knowledge of the energetic system as defined by the seven main chakras. Chakras are by nature difficult to define as they exist in that subtle and invisible realm that surrounds each one of us. However intangible they may appear, there is a grounded logic to the teachings written about them. It is my hope that through my own research, direct experiences and insights I can put together an illustrative guide to Reiki and the seven main energy centres that can be used by any aspiring Reiki healer, to enhance their own healing practice and gain a greater understanding of the subtle anatomy that governs such healing. When we sit down to creatively manifest something in this world, it is my belief that unless that manifestation is supported on an energetic level by Spirit it is very difficult to find a flow of energy to support it. When I sat down to begin this book, I found a real lack of flow in its manifestation. It wasn't until I began to ask Spirit for more clarity as to what this book was about that the energy to support it started to arrive. As so much has already been written about the chakras, this work can never be considered original but rather a collection of ideas and insights from numerous sources. My role as such has been to collate many ideas and views, couple these with my own experiences and present them to you the reader.

What is so amazing about Reiki to me is its capacity to work on so many levels. I have seen, through its simple application, Reiki deliver insights and understanding from the hidden subconscious mind to aid a healing process. I have watched with great compassion as emotional pain has been released, the gentle healing of Reiki inspiring great sobs from deep within a person. I have marvelled at physical symptoms being miraculously healed through simple touch. I have watched people find a new sense of purpose and a renewed vitality for living. I have seen people slowly awaken to a new possibility of living with peace in their own lives and realised the global implications that offers us. What ties all these levels together of course is the chakra system; the present format that Reiki uses to heal is based on these chakras and yet rarely is much written to support that. So here you are – a definitive guide to Reiki and the seven chakras – enjoy.

Introduction:
A Journey To Reiki

"I believe there exists One Supreme Being – the Absolute Infinite – a dynamic force that governs the world and the universe. I shall call it Reiki."

Hawayo Takata

As the pilot of the Hawaiian Airlines flight throttled forward, the tired old DC9's engines vibrated noisily in response like a badly loaded spin drier at full tilt. With a noise to performance ratio severely out of kilter they began to slowly push us forward on our take-off run from Maui airport to the Big Island. Sitting next to me, Thomas was talking about the nature of giving and receiving. He was one of our group that had congregated in Maui for the winter solstice 1996. As we were all far from our families and homes, Alex, a resident of Big Island whom we had met the week before, had invited us over for Christmas. Thomas was explaining universal accountability. "If we ask for a financial exchange for something we teach, we should not be attached to the idea that it has to come from the person we teach it to – it could come from somewhere else," he said, "and not straight away, everything has to balance out." I smiled, thinking how I might persuade my bank manager the merits of this theory next time I asked for a loan!

The DC9 was now up to speed. "Just a moment!" I said, interrupting Thomas. "I need to do something." I placed my hand in front of me and drew the Reiki power symbol in the air. The mantra passed silently through my mind – I visualised the symbol passing down the central isle of the aircraft toward the cockpit. Suddenly the DC9 lurched forward as the pilot urgently applied the brakes the engines that a moment before had been propelling us towards lift-off were hastily throttled back into silence. The aircraft slowed and then turned left off the runway. Out of the right-hand side windows we could see the end of the runway only a hundred yards away and then the ocean. "What did you do? " asked Thomas, looking astonished. "I just remembered what my Reiki master taught me about using one of the Reiki symbols to protect journeys." I said, equally astonished. The Captain came on the intercom and in a customary tone gave us an explanation as if what had just happened was a commonplace occurrence. "Sorry ladies and gentlemen but we need more take-off room for the weight we are carrying. We will taxi to the end of the runway and begin our run from there." I felt the 'telltale tingling of truth' run down my spine and the hair on my arms stood to attention. Sometimes you just know you have experienced a moment of intervention by spirit; a moment where the doorway opens and something reaches through and touches you. It is why we believe in Guardian angels, why in our hearts we know there is someone there watching out for us. It had happened to me before but never in response to something I had done. I knew in my heart that my action of drawing the symbol and the event of the aircraft stopping were connected. Of course it could never be proved and certainly could be argued away, but I knew. So did Thomas.

My interest in Energy had started three years earlier in the September of 1993. After much soul searching and discontent with my life as a photographer in London, I visited the Findhorn community in north Scotland to attend an experience week with 27 others. On my third day there I had been invited to a power point – an area of interconnecting ley lines, similar to energy meridians in the human body – called Venus hill. I was standing in a group of 15 people each holding hands to form a circle. I remember that so much judgement had lifted from me during that day, I found I wanted to participate with the group for the first time. Previously I had been observing them all as strangers with nothing in common with me. Now as we stood there I knew all their names and had connected with each one in some way. I closed my eyes, feeling a sense of expectancy, and a thought passed through my mind – 'Lord use me.'

Jacques, a Parisian who was opposite me, stepped into the circle and held his hands out in front of him, palms down. Suddenly, I knew what I had to do. I stepped forward into the circle and faced him placing my hands underneath his, palms up. At first I felt emotion rising up to my throat and then I started to feel powerful vibrations running up from the ground through me. This created a spiralling sensation below my belly button and I could actually feel the rotation on my skin. It's true that chakras spin and this felt something like a muscle spasm. My throat and jaw became paralysed by the energy so I was unable to speak, and then it seemed to explode through my body forcing great sobs to emanate from deep within me. It was as if I had been plugged into the mains electrical supply and I was aware that I was now experiencing myself as energy, and this energy was tangible far outside my physical body. After a while my jaw freed and I was able to speak "Please take me down from here," I asked one of the group. "I can't take any more!"

Out of the 15 people present that day only Jacques and I felt the energy. Both of us were convinced it was the consequence of the other being present that had generated it. The effect of this experience stayed with us for many days. I had been carrying around so much inner tension for as long as I could remember. It was as if a weight had been lifted from me. I felt cleansed, lighter and purified. The vibrations in my body subsided after a few hours but remained in my hands for a week. I seemed also strangely aware of the feelings of others. I searched for an explanation. I asked many people about what had happened and was offered differing views but none felt quite right to me. What occurred that day showed me that my awareness of the world and the perception I had of it was no longer relevant. I realised that I needed to develop my understanding of this newly discovered world and I set out to find the answers.

Searching For Answers

I spent the year attending seminars and workshops on different forms of healing as well as continuing with my work as a photographer in London. During a visit to the London Mind, Body and Spirit Festival, I happened upon Reiki for the first time. Something about its name interested me though I knew nothing about it. As I approached the stall a friend with me at the time said, "Oh, you don't want to do that, they only care about making money!" Allowing my interest to be countermanded by her opinion, I left without taking any information with me, little realising how significant Reiki was to become in my life.

The following summer my heart yearned for the connection I had felt with Spirit in Findhorn and so I made my way back to Scotland. During the bus ride to Edinburgh the woman sitting next to me had her hands on her heart and solar plexus at one point. "What were you doing?" I asked when she had finished. "Reiki!" she replied. Intrigued, I asked more and she went on to explain what it was. Once in Findhorn, I felt myself once again open to the natural surroundings. The days are beautifully long in summer, with the sun setting briefly into the ocean at midnight in the northwest. Its orange glow is still visible on the horizon until it reappears four hours later out of the ocean a little further east. Time seems to stand still, allowing you to slow down and not feel hurried by the day passing. My stay, as always, was deeply nurturing and through the people I met Reiki began to call to me gently.

On arrival back in London there were two events of significance. Firstly, I received a phone call from a person I had met at Findhorn called Mo asking if I would like to come back up a week later to join her for a Reiki course she had arranged with a master living in the community. Secondly, two letters arrived. The first was information about Reiki, the second a letter from the woman I had met on the bus on the way to Edinburgh. The gentle murmur was becoming a lot more persistent!

My Introduction To Reiki

June Woods, my Reiki master, said, "Place your hand here" and she guided my hand over Mo's solar plexus. At first I felt a tingling sensation then great heat in the palm of my hand. "Are you doing that?" I asked. "No my dear, Reiki is doing that, just relax and let it flow." Those simple words will stay with me forever. It was neither June nor myself creating the flow of energy through my hands, Reiki was, but by me relaxing and letting it flow I was allowing it to happen. I will always feel profoundly grateful that I learned Reiki with June; her approach was always simple, never getting involved in great discussions about it, far preferring a good gossip over a cup of tea and some Battenburg cake. Healing for June was a way of life. She had been a nurse in the Second World War and discovered healing abilities early on, practising through the British Federation of Spiritual Healers for many years before discovering Reiki. 'Indomitable June', as she was affectionately known, was always available whenever asked, and when not healing or running an errand for someone could be found pottering about in her garden with its huge crystal and wind chimes. Her home, a mobile bungalow set in the heart of the Findhorn community near the nature sanctuary, had walls adorned with nick nacks given to her by her many visitors from around the world. She loved dolphins and Native American culture and a picture of Jeronimo looked down proudly at visitors from above the fireplace. Among the many things she introduced to me was Aurasoma – colour vibration essences that work in the auric field. June had a complete set mounted on a clear perspex display cabinet near the window and would always say, "Want a bit of unconditional love dear?" referring to the pink bottle of 'Lady Nada Quintessence'. One of her favourite uses for this aurasoma essence, which is probably not on the Aurasoma list of uses, was to add it to the water in her steam iron before pressing her clothes. Whatever she did it seemed to work and I found her humanity and no nonsense approach to Reiki a great foundation on which I could build.

Becoming A Reiki Teacher

Approximately half a mile from June's bungalow sits RAF Kinloss, a search and rescue facility for antiquated Nimrod aircraft that were a derivative of the Comet, the first commercial jet airliner. These are not the quietest of aircraft, particularly during take-off. It had been a year since I received second level Reiki and on an afternoon in May 1995, the day of my master initiation, they were practising circuits and bumps, which meant every fifteen minutes a great roar could be heard that would shake poor June's bungalow to the core as the Nimrods attempted to break free of Earth's pull. It is at times like these when you find out the level of unconditional love you have managed to attain. "Why today?" I thought – or words to that effect! I was obviously not doing very well.

"Don't worry dear! Just ignore them," said June. "Lets do a little meditation."

Meditation? How on earth was I supposed to be able to meditate with – ROARRRRRR, another Nimrod taking off for another circuit?

"Ask for help!" June said, trying to be heard above the roar.

So as I sat on the sofa, with June's cat curled up next to me, and June opposite in her armchair, we closed our eyes to meditate. "It's no good!" I thought, my mind seizing on this great excuse to sabotage myself, "I am not supposed to become a master. That's it, that's what all this is about!" I attempted to ignore these stray thoughts, settle into my heart and ask the grand masters, Dr Usui, Dr Hayashi, Hawayo Takata to help.

I remember feeling and hearing June stand up; I felt the breeze on my right shoulder and cheek as she brushed past me. She stood behind me and stepped into my body. My breath became rapid as I felt an expansion. Then I felt a guide step into me then another and another, each time an expansion of my being.

When I opened my eyes there was absolute silence. June was looking at me from her armchair, a little concerned. "Are you all right?" she asked. "I had no idea that's how you did it!" I said. "Did what?" June replied, "I haven't started yet, I haven't moved from here." "I have just received the master initiation!" I said and I went on to describe what had happened.

This served to answer all my insecurities about becoming a Reiki master and once again confirmed to me that we just become vehicles for Universal Love. It appears that the process of initiation has little to do with the master giving it. They merely need to be present and act as an anchor for the process to take place.

Later, once I was teaching Reiki myself and passing on initiations, I was always very aware that if the masters didn't choose to turn up, nothing I could do would have much effect. Fortunately for me they have never failed to be present. A recurring vision or insight that many of my students have reported seeing independently of each other has always warmed my heart. This vision is of me placing my hands on their shoulders and behind me Dr Usui placing his right hand on my left shoulder. Behind him Dr Hayashi placing his right hand on Dr Usui's left shoulder and so on with Hawayo Takata, and hundreds of other masters doing the same, forming a train of people until they disappeared into light.

Perception Versus Reality

When I think back to the time I spent in Hawaii, there was an experience I had there that was very similar to the occurrence on the Venus hill in Scotland. I had joined a group that were making their way to the top of Mount Haleakala on Maui for the winter solstice, to meditate and align with the new energies. Our group was charged with expectancy and after driving as far as we could get by car, we set out on foot. After about twenty minutes the focaliser of the group stopped and pointing to a clearing said, "This is the spot." I felt a strong urge to continue and so carried on up the path with the image of the crater vivid in my mind. I soon realised that some of the group were following me, including the group focaliser. By this time wisps of cloud were beginning to obscure the view and the mountain was taking on an otherworldly feel. When I reached the edge of the crater I saw a beautiful piece of grass like a mattress beckoning me to lie down. By now the whole of the mountain was covered in thick cloud and visibility was down to a few metres. I lay down on the earth mattress and almost immediately started to experience strong surges of energy through me. I realised I was once again releasing blocked energy through my central channel. My body was shaking quite violently and several people came to support me through the process, placing their hands over my body to channel healing energy. I was aware of others sitting back and watching. Then the group leader who had taken up position at my head exclaimed, "He has the codes for the ninth dimension!"

The whole experience lasted some 10 to 15 minutes. When I opened my eyes the mist and clouds were gone, replaced by a beautiful blue sky. As I stood up many people came up to me to talk about what had happened. I soon realised that, just as in an accident, you never get two witnesses who saw the same thing, so in this situation people all presented their own version of what they had believed had occurred. The most amusing to me was a man who simply said, "How long have you suffered from epilepsy?" My point in telling this story is that our perception of an occurrence such as this is very much coloured by our beliefs. We all have stories that we believe about reality and we look for experiences that match in order to validate them. Most times they simply aren't true. My body shaking that day on top of that mountain was from my perspective a release, a healing if you like. What the specific cause of that healing was I may never completely understand.

What I do know is that the right set of circumstances came together at a time when I felt open and receptive to healing. This helped me fully trust I could safely release all that I was holding on to. The less attention I give to the event, the less likely I will be caught up in the glamour of it and the quicker I will let go and move on to other experiences. Also it is important to stay with our own feeling about an event. If we get caught up in other people's perceptions of an event, especially surrounding an apparently metaphysical experience, we can become sidetracked by unnecessary drama.

It has been seven years since those first tentative steps with June into the world of Reiki and I have learned much. I know now to be careful not to define myself as a healer and certainly not by the label of master. I have listened to the discontent within the Reiki community and kept my distance. The first thing I had heard about Reiki back in the Mind, Body and Spirit Festival was that practitioners tended to be financially motivated. That is, at times, a justifiable label put on Reiki and an issue that will have to be resolved by the people practising this healing art. But for me, I found I did want to do Reiki, I continue to want to, and the quality of my life as a result and the healing that has taken place is something I am deeply grateful for. I found a doorway through Reiki and it connected me to a part of myself that I often sought; the part that spoke in whispers from within, which called to me gently and warmed my heart again. It is the part of us all that recognises the same search in each one of us; the part that is filled with wonder by the incredible beauty this world offers us. I choose Reiki because I know that it's essence is pure and comes from truth. My experience is that by simply placing my hands on somebody, 'relaxing and letting it flow', something beautiful happens and my life would be much the poorer without it.

Love to you all Richard

What Is Reiki?

"A practice that relieves not only the external, physical sufferings, but the internal sufferings and obscuration of humankind." Dr Usui

The term Reiki is a Japanese word used to describe a system of healing originally known as Usui Shiki Ryoho, or The Usui Way, so titled by its founder Dr Mikao Usui. Though it is difficult to verify the exact events surrounding his life, it appears the system was developed by Dr Usui as a result of a keen personal interest he had in ancient Sanskrit texts and the wealth of information that had been written in them about the energetic bodies and the chakras. Also his deeply felt connection to Spirit led him to research the relationship between the nature of healing miracles and the wisdom of the Sanskrit teachings. In following this personal calling to understand the nature of energy healing, Dr Usui was led to devote his life to the research of what we now know as Reiki. The traditional story we are told is that he received a vision whilst in solitude retreat on Mount Kuri Yama, which revealed to him a unique way to attune people to Universal Ki, the basis of all energy healing. He was shown a series of symbols, written in the sky in gold, each with an accompanying mantra. It was then revealed to him that through the use of these symbols and mantras, placed into Key Chakras within the body in a particular sequence, he could facilitate the opening of a healing channel that would expand through use. Dr Usui developed this practice throughout his life and the Reiki system we know today comes to us unchanged in essence since its humble beginnings at the end of the nineteenth century.

Recently, new information has come to light regarding the discoveries made by Dr Usui, which is said to be taken directly from his original manuscripts. In his manuscripts, translated and published in two books by Buddhist master Lama Yeshe and Reiki master Lawrence Ellyard, Dr Usui writes as the result of his illness with cholera at 27 years of age. He slipped into a dark state of semi-consciousness while in hospital from which he awoke to find himself surrounded by golden light. In this light he saw beings of light that he recognised. They were Mahavairochana, Amida, The Medicine Buddha, Shakyamuni and many Buddha's and Bodhisattvas. He was told that when he recovered from his illness he was to work towards a synthesis of the eastern and western teachings in medicine. When he awoke he found himself in his hospital room and other than weakness, fully recovered. This experience was the beginning of his life's work: to study and perfect the healing system revealed to him by *Shakyamuni Buddha* that had been lost to mankind through carelessness and time. I have included more excerpts from Dr Usui's manuscripts in the chapter 'Reiki A Modern History'.

Reiki has grown to be very popular throughout the world and this is due in part to its simplicity. Reiki is taught as an oral tradition, the basis of which is the transmission of energy from teacher to student known as initiation. The emphasis when learning Reiki is placed on experiencing the energy for oneself. Once a person realises the presence of a universal energy field and their own ability to channel this energy for healing, it is not just a belief instilled in them, it is an experience anchored in them, a deep knowing that stays for life. People today have a greater awareness of alternative means of health care and this includes how they perceive illness and disease. As awareness grows it is understandable that people will gravitate towards preventative medicine, which advocates a way of life rather than waiting for something to go wrong. People will tend to move further and further away from situations that bring them into contact with health advice that makes them feel disempowered. Reiki has been known to bring relief to a range of physical symptoms when other more conventional methods have failed, and because Reiki works on the many levels of a person, the healing can be accompanied by insights as to why the symptoms were created in the first place. It is important to recognise the role of Reiki and other complementary healing practices that could play a more active role in our modern health care systems and could work side by side with them without threatening what already exists.

To best understand the name Reiki we can split it into two parts: Rei & Ki.

The first syllable Rei is Japanese for God, Creator or Spirit.

The second syllable Ki is Japanese for Energy or Power.

Rei – is the term used to describe the creative mind and the creative expression of God, 'all that is', the manifest and unmanifest. The awesomeness of being conscious in a human body and being able to look at space and marvel at the fact you are looking at the past right back to your origins, to 'the big bang'. Everything is 'Rei'; all that you see, smell, taste, touch, feel and hear. Rei is creation and simultaneously you know within your heart that you are part of it; that goes some way to defining Rei.

Ki – is the vital energy that fuels creation, Life Force Energy. Ki powers the motion of the universe. It is the force that animates everything from a field mouse to an exploding star. It is also known in other traditions as *prana* or *chi*. Ki flows through *nadis* or channels in our electromagnetic bodies supplying us, literally, with our life force energy. Using Kirlian photography it is possible to record Ki on film. Interestingly, no matter what you photograph, if it's alive there will always be an electromagnetic energy field around it.

Defining The Essence Of Reiki

In essence Reiki is Love. Whenever I have practised giving Reiki there is a powerful flow of energy into my body, so concentrated that it fills my heart with tremendous warmth. This energy is so tangible that at times it feels like I am literally painting or sculpting with loving light. The analogy of a 'living ocean of energy' is the most accurate definition of the essence of Reiki I have found. What's more, this ocean of energy is an intelligent force. It knows where it is needed the most. Reiki is something anyone can learn to do as we are all intimately connected to the Universe. The ability to give Reiki is learned simply through an oral tradition and a series of initiations from a master to the student. These follow the original teachings founded by Reiki Grand Master Dr Mikao Usui in the nineteenth century. Reiki is a useful tool for self-awareness and personal transformation and will often provide the support for students to release many unwanted issues from the past. Reiki is a non-invasive therapy. There is no need to undress the patient; Reiki works just as effectively through clothes, blankets and in the case of accidents through plaster casts. Reiki can be used in conjunction with many other therapies. Reiki is not affiliated with any religious dogma or practice, enabling people from any religious background to learn it. Reiki is not based on belief, faith or suggestion, rather it is based on the direct experience of those that practice it.

Reiki is:

- A system of energy healing using spiritually guided life-force energy.
- A useful tool for self-awareness and transformation.
- A non-invasive therapy.
- Practised throughout the world.
- A continuation of teachings given by Reiki Grand Master Dr Usui at the end of the last century.
- An honouring of the Dr Usui lineage.
- Used in hospitals, private practice and self-care, and in combination with many other therapies.
- A wonderful complementary healing system on its own or in a personal wellness or healing program.

Reiki is not:

- A religion.
- A cult.
- Affiliated with any religion or religious practice.
- Based on belief, faith or suggestion.

The Famous Five

There are five spiritual principles of Reiki, which were put in place by Dr Usui the founder of the Reiki system. These guidelines are still given today by Reiki masters around the world as a reminder to us of what is of real value. I will build their meanings into the book as I go along, whenever I think of them.

Just for today do not worry
Just for today do not anger
Honour your parents, teachers and elders
Earn your living honestly
Show gratitude to everything

The Lineage

"Life itself is a link in a chain or ripple around the rock in the flow of my stream." Dr Usui

There are many techniques that utilise the transmission of energy to facilitate healing, Reiki being one of them. But what distinguishes Reiki from other systems of energy healing such as spiritual healing, pranatherapy, pranic healing, shen and therapeutic touch? I have met and experienced healing from some very powerful channels throughout the world who have never received a Reiki initiation, and to be honest it was difficult for me to tell the difference in the quality of what I received compared to a Reiki healing. If you look at Dr Usui's experience, he found mention of healing techniques in the texts he read that pre-dated Reiki by thousands of years. Also all systems of energy healing mention the chakra system and energetic bodies in varying depths. I myself felt a need to understand what differentiated Reiki from other techniques and in 1996 I was fortunate to meet Laura, a woman who had been a member of the Federation of Spiritual Healers for over 30 years. She also worked as a medium and so I invited her to receive a Reiki attunement and asked for her feedback. After the attunements she said that the quality of energy was the same as she had been working with for 30 years but at the same time different. The difference was in the guides and helpers who came to support the work; they were completely new to her. Some, she said, appeared to be very ancient masters of healing. She had never met them before and was very grateful for the initiations she received as she now felt a new doorway was open to her.

There are many doorways through which we can step to access and learn how to use energy to heal. It is my understanding from what occurred with Laura that the doorway specific to Reiki connects us to a group of helpers, or guides if you like, that work solely with the Reiki system. This group includes the grand master and founder Dr Mikao Usui, as well as the subsequent grand masters Dr Chujiro Hayashi and Hawayo Takata along with many others. By receiving a Reiki initiation we become connected to this group, they become our healing ancestry, our lineage. Whenever we work with energy, they come to orchestrate the whole healing process. It is not uncommon for people receiving Reiki to comment on experiencing more than one pair of hands on them, even though there is only one person physically in the room at the time. This is an example of these helpers supporting us in our work. What I find fascinating is that these people who have tangibly felt these presences don't always realise that they are not only suggesting the very presence of angelic beings, but have also just had confirmation of their own ability to feel the angelic realms. The introduction of this subtle shift in awareness is to me what is the most exciting part of teaching Reiki. To help people realise that they have just stated quite categorically, "I have felt an angel's hand on my leg"!

Three months after my master initiation, I had an experience that deeply confirmed the relationship between myself and the Reiki lineage and its healing guidance. I was sitting on my bed in Scotland and sure as anything I could feel someone sitting next to me on my right hand side. I sensed this person as great warmth, similar to the heat I experience during healing. I asked within my mind who this person was and the name Takata popped into my head. Normally I would have dismissed this, but the next day I gave a woman called Elvira a healing. She had never received Reiki before and knew nothing about it, but she was well known for her psychic abilities. After the healing she said to me, "Does the name Takata mean anything to you?"

"Yes" I said, "She's the last grand master of Reiki! Why?"

"She is here and wants you to know you are doing a great job and that either she or one of her brothers will always be with you whenever you call on them".

Since receiving Reiki I have increasingly been able to feel the presence of these helpers and find it deeply comforting to know they are around. Often they will arrive whilst I am just going about my ordinary day, as if to remind me they are always there and I am always connected to them. During my time in London, I had my own room in a healing clinic in Chelsea. Each day I would go through the ritual of creating a healing space and called on these helpers. As time went by I found I would arrive in the morning to find that the moment I walked through the door they were there; I no longer needed to call them. The room became so powerful at times, I would watch people coming into that space and see visibly how they were affected by it. I often wondered if I really needed to do anything at all other than talk to them for half an hour, whilst the energy in the room did its work.

Understanding Spirit

"The greatest wisdom seems like stupidity. The greatest eloquence like stuttering." Lin Yutang

Very rarely have I heard a voice speaking directly into my ear and when it has happened, I have usually doubted it. I always wonder if it is just my overactive mind intervening. When I receive clear direction either during a healing or simply in day-to-day life, it manifests as an absolute knowing within me. It always arrives from nowhere, usually when I am not seeking it. The more I search and probe for intuitive flashes or guidance, the more blind I seem to become. There have been exceptions to this but they occurred at times when I seemed to be in one of those graceful episodes of life where my whole existence was infused with the guidance of spirit.

Guidance comes to us in so many ways, sometimes as symbols, sounds, feelings, chance encounters, lyrics of songs and so on. We can actively pursue it by picking a medicine card or meditating on a question, but what is important is our openness to receive. However it comes to us, there has to be that knowing accompanying it, then there is a matching of inner consciousness and outer experience.

Nature is where I feel most connected and Hawaii stands out as a place where I am able to communicate with Spirit and feel the presence of guides at all times. One evening on Maui a dear friend of mine Matthew and I were trying to find a retreat centre where an earth-healing group were staying. As we were operating on a minor budget we had hired an old car and were using it as our hotel. Earlier that day as we wondered how we were going to find this group, I kept feeling we should go to a nudist beach I had heard about. Matthew resisted, thinking I had another agenda! We eventually went and as I was walking down to the beach a dog barked at me. I went over and patted him.

"Is he yours?" I asked a woman lying next to him.
"He belongs to the owner of the retreat centre I am staying at."
she said.
"What centre's that?" I asked.

Bingo! We got the address and set off, as we wanted to join the group for the meditation on Mt Haleakala the following morning. When we got to the approximate area, it was dark and the road we were on was surrounded by thick vegetation. We asked in the nearest town where the retreat was and nobody knew. We were on the right road but had no idea where exactly this place was and the road seemed to go on forever. We pulled over and decided to put our guidance to the test once more. We chose intuitively the direction we felt we needed to go and called on our Reiki guides, saying, "When we get there, please let us know." We drove for maybe

20 minutes and as we came round a corner, in what appeared to be the middle of nowhere, both of us simultaneously shouted out "It's here!" We stopped the car and got out. In the dim glow of the car's headlights we saw a solitary sign carved into a small piece of wood with the name of the retreat centre on it. Now that's what I call guidance!

Initiations

"For I, Usui, am a river. I flow from the past to the future, through many turnings, yet I am that same river, in the past, in the present, in the future."
Dr Usui

To initiate suggests to start something new; in the case of Reiki the initiation is the opening to a new potential, a new way of seeing, feeling and experiencing your life. The initiation forms our connection to a Universal intelligence and the Universal Energy that supports the creation of that intelligence. This first conscious contact with spiritual energy can lead to dramatic changes in how we live our lives and can form the basis of personal transformation and spiritual growth. Many people learn Reiki but not everyone goes on to heal or teach others. Some are content to simply have Reiki in their own lives and use the energy as they interact daily with life.

Whatever our calling, Reiki can provide the catalyst for profound changes and the initiations form the basis of our intimate connection to the Universal Energy that supports those changes.

In all three levels of Reiki, the teacher gives an initiation or sequence of initiations to attune the student to the practical lessons being learned. The teacher giving the initiations, places symbols into the main energy system of the student, concentrating on the crown, third eye, heart and root chakras. He also places symbols into the hands and feet where there are smaller secondary chakras. This enables the student to channel the energy through the hands and remain grounded to the Earth. The master acts as a channel for the energy to pass through himself and the student so that both benefit from the healing flow of energy that passes through them. In my experience, the initiations are powerful healings that act on the central energy channel. As the energy comes in the channel expands and this causes the heart centre to become flooded with energy. This abundance of energy then flows down to the hand chakras.

Depending on the individual being initiated, they may experience strong heat in the heart and down the spine or feel that their body is very heavy. Intense colours may be seen, particularly golds, violets, pinks and greens. They may feel that more than one person is present in the room or the sensation of heat around the shoulders and the feet as if someone were holding them. Visions of faraway places or recollections of being in other places have been reported. Sometimes the grand masters of Reiki are seen connecting to the initiating master. Many experience a deep sense of peace and a reluctance to come back or open their eyes. What each person experiences is unique to him or her. It is also important to remember that for some people, their disposition lends itself to having incredible experiences during the initiation and for others it doesn't, but the ability to channel Reiki does not depend on these experiences.

After an initiation, allow yourself time to integrate it; lie down with your hands on your heart chakra and solar plexus. This helps to keep the energy flowing and allows your system time to adjust. It is not uncommon to feel a little unwell immediately after the initiation, the most common ailment being headaches and nausea. Nearly always the cause of this is a failure to relax and the retention of emotions that wish to surface. If this should occur, you can find relief quickly and effectively by lying on your front and asking someone to place their hands at the top and bottom of your spine. You may feel the movement of energy up and down your spine or small spasms as blocked energy releases through your system. If you experience nausea, lie on your back and ask someone to place his or her hands on your lower abdomen and heart centre. Breathe deeply into your abdomen and relax. You may experience emotions rising up to your throat to be released. The golden rule is that things usually get worse before they get better. So, even if things seem a little intense, try to relax and let go.

Things You Can Experience During And After An Initiation

Seeing vivid colours

Feeling warmth in the heart and hands

Feeling a deep sense of peace

Visions

The need to sleep

Heightened sensitivity

Emotional releases

Pain in the spine and neck

Concepts To Be Dissolved

"From vast emptiness all things have arisen and will return to that same vastness. All things keep on returning. The one permanent thing is the mind of the Buddha, which permeates all existence." Dr Usui

A commonly held belief that does not serve us when we are exploring the energetic world is that, 'nothing exists that we cannot experience with our five senses'. We further enforce this belief if we continue to project it as a pattern on to reality. To truly experience reality we have to first be able to surrender to the idea that reality may communicate to us in ways outside those we are used to experiencing. There are ways that we can help ourselves be more receptive to reality. The simplest is to immerse ourselves in nature because it is real, and if we allow ourselves time to be in it then illusory patterns that we hold within our mind begin to dissolve and fall away. It is all too easy to forget in this busy world of winners and losers we have created for ourselves that it is these very illusions that prevent us resting within and experiencing our true nature.

Our realisation that many things do exist beyond the five senses acts on the emotional body, provoking a response; it begins to awaken. Like the mind that holds rigid belief patterns, the emotional body holds itself in coping patterns. These patterns have been put into place to help deal with the rigid reality we have created for ourselves to live within. If you take away the restricted mental reality it opens the floodgates; the inhibited emotional body, so tightly held together, begins to soften, let go and express itself. Whenever something touches our hearts that reminds us of our true nature, there is an emotional response, and by letting it well up and be expressed it washes and cleanses us without.

First Degree Reiki

"Before practising healing others, it is necessary to heal your own life, to bring stability into your own life." Dr Usui

For many of us, a Reiki class is the first time that we have come into contact with our capacity to heal. Old concepts and beliefs about reality can be challenged during the course, which takes place over a weekend. For this reason, when embraced, the first degree is often experienced as an awakening – a new way of seeing and feeling both ourselves and the environment around us. It is down to the individual how easily this experience is integrated. Reiki One is the start of a journey into the world of energy; consequently, it can help us to let go of rigid thought forms and concepts that may become obstacles to our understanding of this world. Any expectations we may have about what we are going to experience will serve only to block any true experiences that may occur. It is therefore more useful to be open and playful, letting the energy show us how to communicate with it.

The experience of first level Reiki is usually relative to the ability of the participant to let go. I have often thought it best that people know very little about what is going to take place as it prevents them putting together some escape plan. It is our nature to stay in what is comfortable and familiar. When we receive the Reiki initiations, quite often that comfort and familiarity is called into question. This is not to say that Reiki is distressing or foreign, it's just the letting go that we may find difficult.

There is a series of treatments that are learned in Reiki One, which include the full treatment, the short treatment and the self-treatment. These treatments are based around the chakra system and begin with the head and work their way down the body to the feet. By working on the higher chakras first we induce a state of deep mental relaxation in the recipient, akin to sleep. This is not dissimilar to the rapid eye movement (REM) period in our sleep cycle when we dream. In fact most people's closed eyes are highly active during a Reiki treatment and they report seeing inner visions. Once the mind is in this state, it allows the body to relax and is less likely to protect itself and its issues.

When introducing these treatments I always make a point of saying they are guidelines. It is good that we learn these disciplines but not at the expense of our intuition. In time we begin to instinctively know which parts of the body need treating and we should go to them without worrying about the discipline. It is important to listen to these clear signals from our intuition and to learn to trust them. The first degree gives us a simple and safe framework in which to explore energy healing. Once our confidence grows and we learn to feel the movements of energy as we practice these treatments, we can begin to stray from the discipline and explore the energy without the structure. If we get lost, we always have the structure to return to.

Though Reiki is a very powerful tool, I believe the first level weekend should be fun, playful and predominantly an experiential journey into Reiki. It is through direct experience that we come to know something. For this reason, special care should be taken when choosing your Reiki teacher. It is always advisable to receive a treatment from any potential master to decide if you are comfortable with their approach to healing. If so, it is likely that they will have a similar approach to teaching. The main thing is that you feel a rapport with them and your heart feels like it is expanding in their presence. Reiki is very simple and the approach to teaching it should reflect that.

The Energetic Field

"As the light pervades the entire body, one gets attached to the body, mistakes the body for the self and regards the world as different from oneself."
Sri Ramana Gita

According to the theory studied by Dr Usui, the surface vehicles through which we as consciousness express ourselves and interact with the physical world are made up of the physical, etheric, emotional, mental and intuitional bodies, and the will. These six layers range in vibration from the dense physical through to the subtle intuitive layers. These layers are permeated by seven main centres known as chakras, which are focal points for the transfer of Ki energy throughout the whole system.

Part of the function of this energy field is to do with the exchange of sensory input and output. It helps us move and function in the world by providing us with information energetically from within the realms of mind, emotion and physicality. Depending on where the information originates it can range in tangibility from obviously coarse to subtly fine. This interaction takes place on all levels and the surface vehicles are the interface through which that happens.

Anything that is created physically through an action carries an intention behind it, which acts as the motivational force. This force

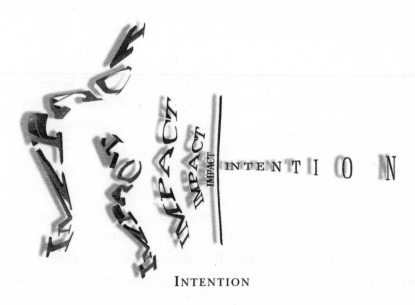

INTENTION

provides momentum and dictates the depth to which that action impacts itself in the physical world. When viewed energetically that intention can be made up of strong beliefs and powerful emotions. When an action is supported by such powerful thought and feeling, what permeates into the physical world through the action is those thoughts and feelings. If the intention is fear-based then the energy that is transferred through the action into the physical world is fear. Conversely, if our intention is loving in nature, this will emanate from us and our actions will be infused with that love.

The Surface Vehicles

THE PHYSICAL BODY

Our physical body is composed of solids, liquids and gases, which together make up the body's systems such as the skeletal, muscular, blood, nervous, lymphatic, immune, digestive and endocrine systems. These all enable the body to function healthily on a day-to-day basis and constitute the denser of the physical functions. The Ki energy that flows through our energetic system determines the vitality of our physical body. A lack of energy flow reaching the physical will result in the vital functions being compromised. The endocrine system matches the positioning of the chakras and is regarded as the vehicle by which energy (Ki) is absorbed or stepped down into the physical body and distributed through the vital organs.

THE ETHERIC BODY

The etheric body carries the flow of Ki through channels known as *nadis* from chakra to chakra. They are like tiny streams that ensure energy flows throughout our system. When the physical body is healthy and full of vitality, this will be reflected in the etheric field around it. An illness in the physical body will show up as gaps or erratic energy flow in the etheric field. The etheric body is affected by our emotional and mental states. If we find ourselves in conflict or depressed, this field of energy will be adversely affected.

THE EMOTIONAL BODY

The emotional body will reflect the immediate emotional charge that is being experienced by a person at the time. If we are feeling happy and joyous or sad and angry our emotional field will reflect that. The emotional body is like a storehouse for both good and bad experiences from our lives, so in addition to immediate emotional experiences, old unresolved patterns are held within this field. Any fear or conflict from the past is retained here and transmitted out to the external world via the chakras as unconscious messages. Consequently, the inner harmony or disharmony of a person is communicated energetically as a result of what is held within the emotional body. In addition, patterns of unconscious behaviour are established and we begin drawing to ourselves people, situations and experiences that reflect our unconscious fears and validate their existence. The world then becomes a mirror for us to observe our unconscious self.

THE MENTAL BODY

In much the same way as the emotional body operates, the mental body reflects our present state of mind; whatever the mind is focused on at a given moment has a powerful affect on how we feel. We deduce from this that the energetic system operates as a whole and not as separate parts. You can test this for yourself right now. Just think about something in your life that has really upset you. As you focus on it, you start to feel upset. The same is true of happy thoughts. Whatever you focus your mind on, impacts on how you feel.

The mind is full of patterns of belief and ideals that are formed throughout our lives. These may reflect our cultural, parental religious and educational inheritance, but they may also be beliefs formed about our capabilities and ourselves. Both the mental and emotional bodies are like transmitters and receivers but the mental body operates at a higher vibration. Thoughts in the conscious and unconscious mind are projected out into the world and, depending on their content, will impact in different ways. The mind can be used to visualise our dreams, visions and aspirations or just as easily our prejudices, intolerance and limitations.

Mental energy is less tangible than emotional energy until we can recognise its signature. If at any time you have journeyed into a large city after a period of rest in nature you may have observed how your mind, which had been so clear, starts to become cluttered by odd thoughts. It's as if a mental invasion takes place, an overload, as we are bombarded with sensory input. A short stay in a large city demonstrates the tangible nature of subtle mental input. We begin having thoughts that really don't sound like our own, and if we stay longer a constant background chatter of disturbing thought will replace our quiet minds.

What we are experiencing here is the human mind's capacity to receive the prominent thought forms around us. It is important to be vigilant as to what thoughts we are absorbing. If you spend the day focusing entirely on all the world's problems, reading papers and watching the news, that is what will make up your mental field. The mind is a powerful vehicle and it is advisable to reclaim ownership of your own mind by being aware of what you allow into it.

THE VOLITIONAL (WILL) BODY

The will body is not often included in subtle anatomy. Some theories suggest the front chakras are the feeling centres and the back chakras the will centres. Our will is the energy we summon to maintain our focus on a given task. It is what makes a marathon runner sprint the last two hundred metres of the race to win. Our will can overcome physical, emotional and mental limitations to help us achieve a goal. It is the holder of choice and as such linked to the ego.

THE INTUITIONAL BODY

The intuitional body receives input by more subtle means; information that enters in this way will often appear as an inner knowing. A flash or picture often accompanies these intuitive feelings and we just suddenly know something without any rational understanding of how. When we act upon intuition we are often amazed at the apparent synchronistic effect it has on our lives. When we choose not to listen to these impulses we always wish we had. The process of interpreting the information coming from our intuition involves us being receptive. We have to listen to those gut feelings, follow the signs given to us and have the courage to act on impulses that our rational mind thinks are foolish. When we talk of someone being highly intuitive it simply means they are paying attention to the signals that are coming in from this energetic body. We all have the capacity to be intuitive but many of us don't listen or trust what we feel.

Melding

One day I was watching a nature program on television showing turtles that had found their way back to this one beach to lay their eggs. Once the eggs hatched, the young turtles would swim out to sea and not return until they too were adults and were ready to lay their eggs. Why is it that only humans need maps? Can you imagine a turtle stopping to ask for directions? The truth is we all operate so much through our rational mind these days that our intuitive instincts are often ignored, although we do rely on them more than we may at first realise, especially when we are in an unfamiliar environment. When our physical surroundings change, the energy that makes up those surroundings changes with them. Different countries have different languages, climates, cultures, foods, customs, belief systems and emotional interactions. Different areas of the earth have qualities peculiar to them; east Africa is literally another world compared to the south of England. The rich cocktails presented to us when we first find ourselves in another environment bombard our senses. Subtly our behaviour begins to change. Our body language mimics the body language of those around us in an effort to fit in. If we can't speak the language we rely on eye contact, gestures and humour to be understood. We begin to rely on instinct and the information coming from our intuition. We smell food before eating it, we orientate ourselves by exploring our environment. Bit by bit we become more comfortable as we settle into the rhythms of our new surroundings. This process I call 'Melding'. We do it constantly without necessarily realising it. In time, we may be introduced to new beliefs that dissolve old outdated ones or experience new emotions. When we return to our homes, we are suddenly aware of how we have changed. What was once familiar is now strange. Once again we intuitively feel out our original surroundings and meld back into them. This is a natural process of harmonising with our environment, relying on our intuitive and instinctive nature to communicate with our surroundings. If we live in the country we will become countrified, if we go to the city we will become urban creatures. This form of subtle communication occurs energetically and it can be refined into a highly sensitive tool by which we can navigate our way through our surroundings.

Communicating With Fields Of Energy

Have you ever seen jelly fish that pulse and as they do a wave of colour runs through them from the inside to the outside? Well, every time we feel, think or want something, imagine that a similar pulse is sent out from us energetically. Whether we are sensitive, angry, sad, happy, needy, sexy, tired, aggressive, indifferent, controlling, depressed, fearful, mad or bored, people around us will always sense it because that's what we are telling them energetically. Anything that presently occupies the energetic bodies will be what is communicated, so when we meet someone, aside from relating to them physically with our five senses, communication on a subtle level is also taking place. This is the good vibe, bad vibe feeling we get about someone. When we feel good about ourselves, the pulse that is sent out communicates this to those around us. If we are really angry our whole subtle body is saying: 'Red alert! Stay away! I could explode if provoked!' Everybody feels this. Even if they don't associate these feelings with their ability to feel subtle energy, that is precisely what they are doing.

Developing A Real Sense Of Yourself

"How did the great rivers and seas get their kingship over the hundred lesser streams? Through the merit of being lower than they; that was how they got their kingship." Lin Yutang

Being able to 'see' auras is only surpassed by levitating or walking on water in the spiritual searcher's list of must dos! I jest, but it is one of those gifts sought after by a huge proportion of the seekers in this world. Why? Perhaps, it is so that they can feel more powerful? If someone says they can see aura everyone wants to know what theirs is like. If such a person were to come up to you and say you have a really dark energy field, it could really upset your day and how would you know any different? Is that useful? Unfortunately, for the majority, when dealing with these subtle realms we rely somewhat naively on information received externally and it need not necessarily be true just because someone claims to be able to see your energy field. Developing our intuitive senses is about learning to listen and trust our own impulses a little bit more. Our capacity to experience the subtle world around us is limited, because the modern world doesn't give much credibility to it. We spend our formative years developing our rational minds. My school never introduced subtle anatomy to me. We never had dowsing classes, chakra workshops, crystal workshops, massage courses, or meditation classes when I was a lad. Yet for a child who is wide open and so full of questions, would it not be more sensible to balance the curriculum with alternatives? By developing a little understanding of the function of our subtle bodies we can start to appreciate that we have always had the ability to sense energy.

A Personal Investment

Throughout our lives we have experiences that when collected together define who we are. Our energetic bodies are like a treasure chest, containing everything that we have chosen to keep for ourselves on this journey we call life. Every memory, every occurrence, every hurt, every joy, all we have learned and remembered, is put together and becomes who we are. We pack our chests full, believing they need to be full or we won't be anybody. Whenever we meet someone, this is what we use to describe ourselves. How much of what is in the treasure chest represents who we really are? Do we feel truly comfortable knowing these collected memories, events, emotions and histories are what define us? Sometimes we need to lift the lid off our treasure chests and take a look inside. Everything in it takes up space, and uses energy to keep it there. Maybe we no longer need some of it and could throw it away, leaving more space, more room for newness to flow in?

Photographing The Invisible

Because the energetic field is electromagnetic in structure, it is possible to record an image of it on film. There have been various techniques developed to photograph it, including Auric, Kirlian photography and the Gas Discharge Visualisation machine invented

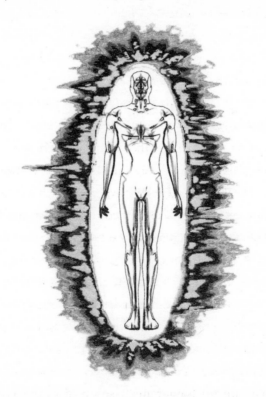

AN EXAMPLE OF A BALANCED ENERGY FIELD

by Dr. K. Korotkov in Russia. The images produced show an egg-like energy field surrounding the physical body. This is usually made up of several different colours that are deemed to reflect the emotional, mental and physical energy the person is presently experiencing. If you were to take several pictures of your own energy field within a short period of time you would see that this field of energy is constantly changing, depending on the current influences around it. This is useful as it helps us to view ourselves as living in a world of energy that is in constant flux rather than just a world of solid structure. Seeing this helps us realise our daily interactions within this world of energy affects us moment to moment.

Letting Go To healing

In Reiki we are concerned with two main aspects of the energy field. Firstly, it is essential that we become aware of what it is that we have chosen to hold within our energy fields, which creates restriction and causes continued suffering. This can take the form of beliefs on the mental level, trauma on the emotional level and, more often than not, distortion on the intuitive level. Through the application of Reiki we can gently introduce a harmonious energy into the system. This has the effect of highlighting the areas in the various surface vehicles that are holding disharmonious energy. When a melodious energy meets a dissonant one, it very gently reminds it how to be tuneful. Secondly, we can become aware of how our energy interacts on a day-to-day level with the energy fields of those around us. Once we have come to know our own system we begin to see how our experiences are like patterns that repeat themselves as a result of what we are sending out into the world as unconscious messages. We may wonder why certain situations keep arising in our lives, but it is only when we become aware of our unconscious projections that we can stop these patterns repeating.

The Knots In Our System

What are knots in the system? In simplistic terms a knot is a distorted pattern within you that you are holding onto; that separates you from reality and that could be released. It can be a belief, an idea, a religion, an emotion, a need, a want, a path, a feeling, a pain, an expectation, insecurity, control, or survival issues. The action of holding onto anything creates a contraction within your energetic bodies that, wherever it is located, obstructs the free flow of energy throughout your system. The contraction can occur in the mind as a thought or idea or belief. It can occur in the emotions as a feeling or a need or in the body as a pain or disease.

Any past issue we are still reliving wastes precious Ki energy that could be used in our present either physically, in maintaining our health and well-being, or creatively, in manifesting whatever it is we wish for ourselves, even healing others. Have you ever had an emotional conflict with someone, and whilst they are no longer around and you can't see them you still keep focusing on the conflict, playing it over and over in your mind? How exhausting is that? All that Ki focused negatively towards that person! You feel like you have no energy to do anything else. The moment you resolve the conflict, hey presto, you feel 100 per cent better. Whatever the drama – fear, anger,

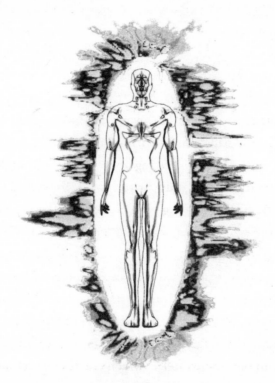

AN EXAMPLE OF A DISRUPTED ENERGY FIELD

pain, addiction, jealousy, depression, conflict, attachment – it sits like a dark cloud in your energy field, draining away your life force and it costs you a percentage of your energy! We have hundreds of these conflicts that remain unresolved and sit in our energy fields like scars. Think about it! How often do you use the past as an excuse for present failures? You may even do so unconsciously. Listen to your mind. How often when you are trying to improve yourself in any way do you hear it giving you reasons not to continue? The voice you hear may be that of your father, mother or teacher but it is now in you – you held on to it, believed it, embraced it and continue to use it as an excuse. The same is true of your emotional body. Any time you are presented with a new challenge, observe how your emotional field contracts in response. Chakras will close down, disabling and disarming you so you are less effective. When a healing space is held through the use of Reiki, it offers the opportunity for release. It simply and very tenderly says, "It's OK, you can let go!" The acuity of this release will be proportional to how much is being held and for how long. For example, my experience on the power point was intense because I had held onto so many issues for so long and none of it was real, none of it served me at all. The only thing that really serves us is to let go, the only healing is to let go. Release ultimately cures everything.

It is fundamental that we become aware of what we have chosen to hold within our energy fields, which creates restriction and causes continued suffering. The trick in healing is to discern where the distortion occurs. For this to be accurate we need to hone our subtle skills and couple this with a deeper knowledge of the seven main energy centres.

The Chakras

In Reiki, the treatments we give focus on seven main points within the energy field known as *chakras*. In Sanskrit, chakra means wheel or disc and this serves to describe the spinning motion that chakras employ to store, regulate and distribute Ki (life force energy) into our subtle and physical bodies. The root or base chakra is the first of these distribution points, and is found at the base of the spine, at the perineum. As its name suggests this chakra acts as our connection to the Earth and a base that the rest of the chakra system is built upon. From this base run three principal channels through which the energy flows. These channels are known as *Ida, Pingala* and *Sushumna*. Sushumna runs vertically up from the base chakra to the crown chakra and these two chakras open up at each end to form our connection to both earth and spirit. Ida and Pingala spiral upwards in opposite directions from the root chakra intersecting along the length of this vertical channel to form five horizontal chakras where they meet, each one having a direct relationship both physically and subtly to the part of the body it governs.

These three main distribution channels carry the energy between the chakras and also to the finer channels known as *nadis*.

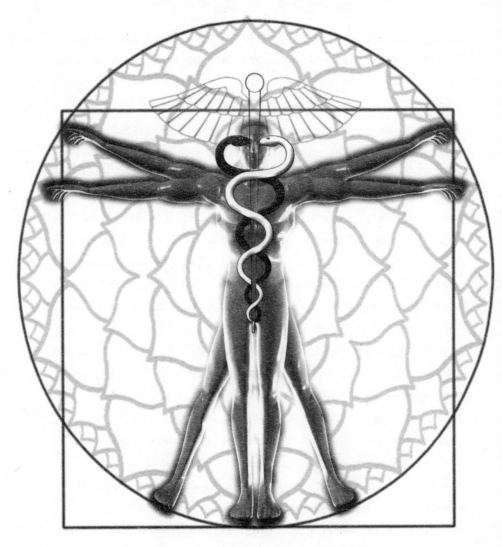

JOURNEY OF IDA AND PINGALA

These can be likened to arteries and veins that carry blood pumped from the heart throughout the physical body; in this case however, the nadis are carrying vital energy. Three main vehicles – the creative mind of the body, the endocrine system and the nervous system – step down this energy or Ki for use in the physical body. The creative mind is the intelligence contained within every living cell; it enables the body to function healthily running all of its systems on apparent autopilot, until of course something goes wrong! The endocrine system produces hormones that regulate a number of bodily functions, all of which are vital to our physical development and health. The nervous system provides us with our link to the physical world through the individual mind and the five senses.

From a Reiki viewpoint, disease begins when there is a disturbance to the flow of universal life force energy along any of these pathways. This disturbance can exist at any point between the chakras and one of the three vehicles that distribute the energy, thereby causing a lack of energy in the physical body leading to a physical ailment or disease. The source of these disturbances is invariably found to originate in the realms of emotion, mind and will. Healing always requires the person who created the turmoil to let it go.

The fact that we focus on seven main energy centres appears in keeping with natural rhythm. The colours of these seven centres correspond to the seven colours of the rainbow, the component parts revealed when a ray of white light is dispersed by refraction through a water droplet or a glass prism. Refraction occurs because the different wavelengths of the colours are dispersed at different angles as they enter the water droplet or prism. The colours red, orange, yellow, green, blue, indigo and violet are called the spectrum of white light. In chakra theory these same seven colours are each attributed to a chakra, beginning with the colour red at the base chakra and ending with violet at the crown. Seven appears throughout nature as a recurring theme. There are seven notes on a musical scale, referring to a range of sound frequencies this time. These are used in chakra balancing therapies to help reharmonise the chakra system in the form of toning or the playing of instruments like the didgeridoo.

It is believed that as we evolve within the physical body, the concentration of Ki moves up from the base through the various chakras, becoming higher in vibration as it ascends. Each chakra is like a string on a guitar tuned to a different frequency (reflected in the colours of the rainbow). Each chakra contains information relevant to its vibration. The physical, emotional and psychological aspects assigned to each chakra represent a journey, a progression through life. This journey begins in the base chakra and moves through the lower chakras that operate in denser frequencies. As consciousness we develop through experiencing basic issues such as survival, trust, security, reproduction, self worth, identity, power, control and relationships. As we evolve through life and integrate these experiences, more Ki is available to be raised up to the higher chakras and the issues become lighter. We start to develop understanding about compassion, healing, creativity, mindfulness and our divine consciousness. It is important to note that just because we refer to the lower chakras as having a denser frequency, this does not mean they are bad. As consciousness we have the potential to develop both positively or negatively any of the chakra aspects we pass through.

There are differing schools of thought as to the time each phase of development occurs in our life. Some suggest this progression through the chakras occurs in seven-year phases from the time of birth, starting with the base. At the end of each seven-year cycle we as consciousness are said to graduate to the next chakra, where we spend the next seven years integrating its particular aspects. During each seven-year phase along with the development of the relevant chakra, there is said to be the influence of one other chakra depending on which year. For example in our eighth year we will be in the development phase of the 2nd chakra but also have the influence of the 1st chakra, and in the tenth year we will again be in the development phase of the 2nd chakra and also have the influence of the 3rd chakra. Seen this way, the journey through the chakras is a simple progression, each year symbolising a phase of development. Once we have reached the end of the development phase for the 7th chakra, we move back to the 1st chakra and repeat the process over again.

Another school of thought is that this progression starts in the 1st chakra at conception, and develops through to the end of our first year or until as a baby we can stand and walk on our own. We then move into the 2nd chakra until our second year. This period is about us moving independently, being able to experience the world and developing our sensory experience. Then we move into the 3rd chakra from our second year and begin to develop our independent will and power. The 4th chakra is developed from our fourth year to our sixth year and here we develop our understanding of giving and receiving and issues of relating to others. At seven years old we move into our 5th chakra and develop our ability to communicate and express ourselves. In our twelfth year we move into our 6th chakra and develop our memories, our intuitive and intellectual mind and our inner and outer perception. Finally, at twenty we move into our 7th chakra and here we integrate our experiences and develop inner wisdom. This is seen as the formative development of the chakra system. From here as adults we repeat the cycle through the chakras again.

Our progression through the chakras in a given lifetime will depend greatly on the willingness of each consciousness to evolve and also on the outside influences of family environment and culture we find ourselves in. If as consciousness, we are conceived into a family environment or culture that is heavily influenced by the energy of the lower chakras and has become stuck or entrenched in their negative aspects, it will appear more challenging for us to evolve beyond these influences into the more positive aspects and raise our Ki energy into the higher chakras. This explains why a consciousness born into a family in a country which has been in conflict for generations with its neighbours can inherit the beliefs that fuel the conflict. We say we love our children, but if that were true why do we ask them to carry the same burdens that we have carried and been restricted by? If our love for our children is genuine, would we ask them to replace their wide-eyed innocence with our prejudices? Unless a consciousness remembers it is only born into a culture and is free to disagree with the ideologies within it, there is the danger it will become stuck there.

If you look at the news you will see there are thousands of examples of this worldwide. If we free ourselves from beliefs and ideologies that cause anger and resentment, our children will be spared from having to carry them too.

There is a certain ambiguity in chakra development theory and though I have listed two examples to try and give some understanding to their formation, it is the characteristics of each chakra that I wish to focus on. Whichever model of chakra development is followed, it is clear that the development of our psyche and emotional nature, takes place primarily in the

BUILDING BLOCKS   formative period of our lives. In order to heal and resolve any issues and blocks that may restrict us we need to look to these periods in some way to heal them. Imagine the building blocks that children play with. Each block needs to be aligned with the one below to ensure the whole stack is balanced correctly and doesn't fall down. If one is placed incorrectly it affects the other blocks on top of it and they will have to compensate in order to balance the stack. Each block placed on such a stack will have to compensate more and more as the imbalance will increase the higher the stack is built. To correct an imbalance one always has to go down to the offending block that is causing the instability throughout. Once realigned, each block above can also be brought back into alignment.

In giving Reiki, an understanding of the aspects of each chakra can be of great value, as patterns of emotional or psychological behaviour are assigned to particular chakras. This can help us to target the correct area of the energy field when giving a treatment. We have to be cautious though of pigeon-holing people and their issues. Just like the treatments in Reiki provide us with a structure in which to work, the chakra system is a map of the human energy system that can be referred to as a guide. It is not our job to diagnose or give spiritual or psychological counselling unless we have training that qualifies us to do so. An understanding of the chakra system gives us an insight into the way the human energy field operates and this can be a useful aide to our work. As Reiki flows to where it is needed most, we get good feedback if we target the correct areas. Suddenly, because it is needed, there will be a rush of energy through us to that area. So as we begin to integrate chakra theory into our work, Reiki should be the teacher. If you are correct in your assumption that a chakra is in need of balancing, Reiki will flow strongly through you to confirm what you felt.

The Seven Main Chakras At A Glance

1st Chakra

MULADHARA meaning 'root of our support'

Commonly known as the base centre

Location perineum, base of spine

Colour Red

Element Earth

Governs The kidneys, adrenals, pelvis, hips, knees, lower back, sciatic nerve, bowel movement

Traditional development ages: 0-7 years

BALANCED

Earthly abundance, prosperity, trust in the natural flow of life, stability, ability to relax, health, vitality, ability to let go, sharing, supporting and sustaining the planet and its inhabitants, security, feeling at home, eating slowly, physical and mental flexibility, generosity, optimism.

IMBALANCED

Addiction to security, rigid boundaries, hoarding, attachment to material security, greed, stealing, gulping food, obesity, pessimism, waste, vandalism, stagnation, fear of the future and the ability to survive, self-absorption, instability, restlessness, homelessness, escapism, excessive financial worry, poverty, underweight, constipation and low energy.

2nd Chakra

SVADHISTANA meaning 'your own dwelling place'

Commonly known as the sexual centre

Location between the genitals and naval

Colour Orange

Element Water

Governs The genitals, reproductive organs, bladder and prostate

Traditional development ages: 7-14 years

BALANCED

Fluidity, creativity, self-esteem, knowledge of where you come from (dwelling place) and where you are going, receptivity, freedom, fertility, desire, pleasure, sensuality, sexual health, intimacy, reproduction, emotional balance and ability to give and receive from the wellspring of life.

IMBALANCED

Sex addiction, manipulation, emotional immaturity, jealousy, sexual abuse, obsessive attachments, poor boundaries, the sending of mixed messages, lack of fluidity, competitiveness, victim consciousness, blocked creativity, feeling unloved, sexual abuse, inability to be intimate, rigidity, fear of pleasure, emotional numbness, frigidity, impotence, genital problems, lower back problems, the holding of physical, emotional and energetic toxicity in the lower body.

3rd Chakra

MANIPURA meaning 'dwelling place of jewels'

Commonly known as the power centre

Location at the solar plexus

Colour Yellow

Element Fire

Governs The spleen, liver, gall bladder, stomach and pancreas

Traditional development ages: 14-21 years

BALANCED

A strong sense of identity without the need to dominate others, vitality, spontaneity, strength of will, sense of purpose and self-esteem.

IMBALANCED

The need to dominate others, seeing yourself as separate from others, judgemental, critical, aggressive, blaming, overly active and defensive, weak-willed, poor self-esteem, over-passivity, fearfulness, sluggishness, hypersensitivity, nervous tummy and anger turned inward.

4th Chakra

ANAHATA meaning 'that which is ever new'

Commonly known as the heart centre

Location at the centre of the chest

Colour Emerald Green

Element Air

Governs The physical heart, lungs and thymus

Traditional development ages: 21-28 years

BALANCED

Compassion, self-acceptance, healthy relationships, internal balance.

IMBALANCED

Co-dependency, setting poor boundaries, possessiveness, jealousy, shyness, loneliness, isolation, bitterness, being critical, lacking empathy, asthma, heart disease and circulatory problems.

5th Chakra

VISHUDDHA meaning 'purest of the pure'

Commonly known as the throat centre

Location at the throat

Colour Sky Blue

Element Ether or Space

Governs The vocal chords, thyroid and voice

Traditional development: ages 28-35 years

BALANCED

Clear communication, creativity, freedom of expression.

IMBALANCED

Excessive talking, inability to listen, stuttering, fear of speaking, poor rhythm, thyroid diseases, sore throats and general throat problems.

6th Chakra

AJNA meaning 'command'

Commonly known as the third eye

Location on the forehead between the eyebrows

Colour Indigo

Element Light

Governs The pituitary gland

Traditional development: ages 35-42 years

BALANCED

Psychic perception, accurate interpretation, imagination, clear vision.

IMBALANCED

Nightmares, hallucinations, delusions, difficulty concentrating, poor memory, poor vision, denial, headaches.

7th Chakra

SAHASRARA meaning 'thousand-petalled lotus'

Commonly known as the crown centre

Location at the crown of the head

Colour White or Gold

Governs The pineal gland

Traditional development: ages 42-49 years

BALANCED

Wisdom, knowledge, consciousness, spiritual connection.

IMBALANCED

Over-intellectualism, spiritual addiction, confusion, dissociation, scepticism, limiting beliefs, materialism, apathy.

The Seven Chakras In Depth

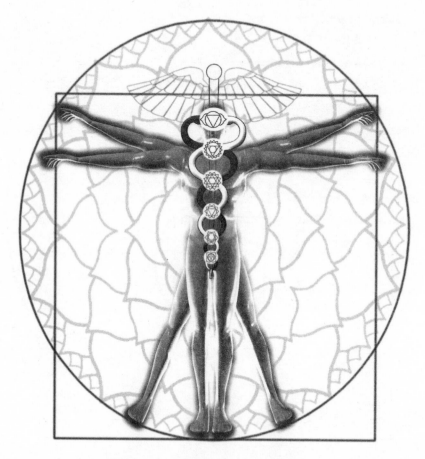

THE COMPLETE CHAKRA SYSTEM

1st Chakra: Muladhara

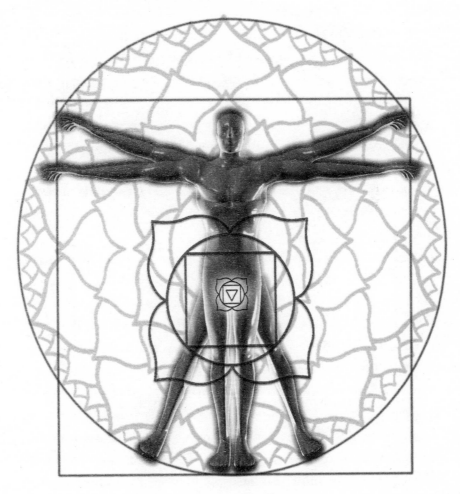

ROOT CHAKRA

Our journey through the seven stages of the chakra system begins here in the Muladhara chakra. It is situated at the perineum between the genitals and the anus. When we look at a tree we know that its roots penetrate deeply into the earth, enabling the tree to survive the elements above the ground by ensuring a stable base. These same roots also provide the necessary nutrients for the tree's health and survival. But we too require a root system to develop a healthy connection to the earth. The journey through the first chakra enables us to fulfil our primary requirements for basic survival. By developing a strong root system we are also building a strong platform on which to stand in order to weather the various storms life might throw at us.

Just as foundations determine the structure and design of any building upon them, the first chakra is the foundation for the entire chakra system. Any weakness or instability in the base chakra will have a knock-on effect throughout the rest of the system. Our connection to the earth begins at conception and continues through the gestation period in our mother's womb. We begin experiencing the world through our mother, for every sound, movement, thought or feeling we have is a direct result of what our mother is experiencing in the outside world. We depend on this relationship for our survival and it sets the pattern for us to develop our own connection once we are born to another mother, the Earth.

If during the formation of our foundations we are surrounded by conflict, we won't feel safe and the energy that could be channelled into our continued development is used to fuel our basic need to survive. Whenever we are faced with something that threatens our survival, our attention becomes focused only on that. If the first chakra is developed within a climate of uncertainty, a range of issues can surface physically, mentally and emotionally which affect our general well-being and anything we do becomes undermined by a *Basic* feeling of unease.

The Muladhara chakra means 'root' and this explains the function it has across all levels of our being. It relates to our physical connection to the Earth and the nourishment we receive. The food we eat, the water we drink, the air we breathe, the aromas we smell, and the things we touch and see. Energetically we are rooted to the Earth; our chakra system is 'plugged' into a larger planetary system, which in turn is connected to the solar system and the whole universe. Our ability to ground ourselves brings us into the present moment in time and space. This is vital for us if we are to have a healthy relationship to reality. If we cannot stay 'present' we will always drift around in illusory states that we come to believe are real. We will be susceptible to outside influence and will lose contact with what we instinctively know to be true, preferring instead to believe the information we receive from without. The base chakra provides us with the essential characteristics to manifest not only our basic needs, but also our dreams and ideas. This connection to the physical world offers us the materials and parameters within which we can build and create. Through a healthy connection to the Earth we develop a firm footing. We learn to declare our boundaries and develop responsibility. We are ready to turn obstacles into challenges that we are willing to face and we stay true to what we are and know. We become unshakeable.

Whilst trust represents a healthy aspect of the first chakra, fear erodes it, leading to contraction and the restriction of the life force. Fear undermines all the healthy states of the base chakra, which are safety, security, trust, health and solidity, causing weakness in our foundations that wastes precious energy. Fear prevents us being in a healthy state of inner relaxation by paralysing us and disconnecting us from the Earth which provides us with our basic needs. Any survival fears we may have originate in the first years of our life. As a baby or young child we are very much reliant on our parents, surroundings and environment for the basic needs of life such as shelter, food and love. As most of the patterns of fear have existed for generations and generations, our formative years are influenced greatly by these survival issues. If our parents worry about where the next meal is coming from or how to meet the monthly bills, as children we are affected. Later in life, as adults, we may earn good salaries and live in a nice home yet still we may be anxious about meeting our monthly expenses and will have a sense that we don't have enough. Subconsciously we are still plugged into unnecessary survival issues from our childhood and they create instability in our foundations. Consequently, Ki, which could be channelled positively into feelings of abundance and prosperity, is being blocked or wasted on our subconscious fears. Any time we have a strong desire to achieve something – an idea, a dream – an argument will be offered up from a deep fracture within us that prevents the grounding of that idea or dream. It's a little like trying to wade through waist-deep mud whilst carrying somebody on your back. Never underestimate the disabling effect of deeply ingrained negative thoughts and feelings on day-to-day life. Anything built on foundations affected by underlying fears will be prone to crumble.

KUNDALINI

The first chakra is the home of the Kundalini, the mythological serpent that lies coiled up asleep at the base of the spine. Kundalini represents the primal force that can rise up through the chakras, bringing about shifts in consciousness and sudden awakenings. In a way the Kundalini is the condensed life force contained within the seed of our potential. If that energy is released then we can flower as consciousness. The circumstances that lead to the release of this energy can be varied. Traditionally, the awakening of the Kundalini is seen as a result of work being done on the chakra system through various disciplines. When a level of balance is achieved it enables the energy to rise. There are yoga disciplines specifically designed with this task in mind and they have become popular in the western world.

A degree of caution should always be observed in releasing this energy. If it is done before we are ready, there is a danger that we may lose our connection to the earth and become ungrounded. This, in turn, can lead to disorientated states of consciousness as energy becomes concentrated in the higher chakras.

I have experienced these rushes of energy through my system in various ways; the most powerful occasion was on the energy point in Forres, Scotland. The experience can be unpleasant and frightening as the energies involved are incredibly powerful. What I have learned from my experiences is that once this energy rushes through the system, it is important to maintain contact with the earth and allow the energy that has risen up through the channels to filter back down to the ground. I remember feeling very high on this energy and at times thought I wouldn't be able to get back into my body. I found the most useful grounding tool was to chop and stack wood for a week. I also made sure I spent time being quiet and gentle.

Kundalini releases can occur in far less dramatic ways. Any time you feel fidgety or restless the likely cause is Kundalini, but this restlessness can be resolved by taking some exercise or by receiving massage. During Reiki sessions it is common for peoples' bodies to jump or spasm and, again, this is Kundalini energy firing through the nadis or channels and is quite normal.

HURT PEOPLE HURT PEOPLE

Melvyn was a sensitive man, though he didn't trust his own perceptions. He would often defer to others and ask what they thought and what they wanted. He would seek out tarot readers or clairvoyants and find himself constantly deferring to people with apparent authority on a whole range of issues. He was always giving away his power to others. When I first gave him a Reiki treatment and came to his lower back, I placed my hands on his coccyx and there was an immediate and powerful emotional response. From deep within his psyche a memory had surfaced that was obviously buried a long time ago. He recalled seeing himself as an 11-year-old boy being beaten by a teacher with a size 14 gym shoe in a basement shower room wearing nothing but a pair of swimming trunks. Nobody else was there and the teacher was shouting at him to "Take it like a man". As he relived this experience a lot of anger and hatred towards the teacher surfaced because he felt abused. Subsequently, he spent many years working on the issue-which included going back to the school and sitting in the shower room to try to understand what had happened. The anger, though, remained.

Seven years later he was going through the break up of a long-term relationship. The issue that affected him more than any other was that his partner had lied to him and he had allowed himself to be manipulated, causing him to see events from her perspective rather than his own. He had always known within that what he was hearing from her was not always the truth, but he didn't trust his own intuition. Instead he chose to trust her even when it came to his own personal decisions. He deferred to her on all levels, projecting on to her purity and wholeness, all the while believing himself to be impure. Once he learned about the lies, he no longer knew what was true and what was false. He couldn't fall back on his own truth because he had denied it for so long. After a lot of hurt, anger and pain what emerged into his awareness was that he had no personal authority. He realised he had to reclaim his power and to do that he had to forgive the teacher in the shower room. He eventually saw that even though he had appeared defenceless as an 11-year-old boy, he had still had a choice and he had chosen to accept the distorted authority over his own, and the ensuing punishment. Forgiveness came when he understood that at some time in the past, during the teacher's childhood, he had probably experienced something similar. The pattern of dysfunction that had passed through him had probably existed for generations and generations in different ways in others. Now there was the opportunity for that pattern to die in him, and in so doing free him. From understanding the pattern and learning to forgive he was able to rebuild his foundations and develop trust in his own authority again.

For me it clarified how patterns can be passed from person to person through the subconscious intent behind the action. The beating was the action that carried the pattern from the teacher to the

11-year-old boy. The reason that it penetrated so deeply into his psyche and affected him in such a disabling way was because it was delivered with such intent and in such a violent manner directly into his first chakra, the characteristic of which is *Trust*. This manifested itself in Melvyn primarily as a lack of trust in himself; he didn't trust his feelings, his intuitions, his opinions, his decisions, his abilities and so on. In other words, every chakra had been affected by the instability caused in the base chakra.

IMBALANCES

One of Dr Usui's principles was '*Earn your living honestly.*' This means to make a living in ways that support and sustain the Earth and its inhabitants rather than through means that deplete and diminish them. Another of his principles was '*Just for today do not worry.*' These principles refer to the first chakra and ask us to trust in the natural flow of life and be secure in the knowledge that our needs will be met. If we examine the effect that an unstable foundation can have on our lives, we will see that our disconnection through the base chakra massively affects our relationship to the earth. Signs of imbalance can be found by simply walking down a busy street in any major city. Litter boxes overflow with discarded packages; people in expensive cars stuck in congestion throw cigarette butts out the window; homeless people lie curled up in sleeping bags in shop doorways begging for food. People selling life insurance, health insurance, mortgages, 'buy now pay later', 'save for the future', capitalise on the message of security and safety in a dangerous world. There is a relentless strive for more and more. Prejudice, muggings, theft, abuse and addiction thrive. Wars, conflicts, famine and floods seem commonplace. TV news programmes disclose the most recent disasters or inquiries into the latest train crash. People ask, 'Why? How could it happen? Why aren't we safe?' And yet we still cut down forests, sell water, pollute the air, litter space, genetically modify our crops and build huge concrete monstrosities to show that we are no longer in contact with the Earth.

In writing this chapter I have come to realise that without a healthy base chakra there is little point in developing any other chakra. So much emphasis is placed on opening the third eye and on developing our psychic and healing capabilities, but little thought is given to ensuring the root system is first in place. If you just do one exercise each day, let it be to ground yourself. Our physical bodies are the temples within which the sacred can be expressed. The physical body never lies; it will always tell you what is going on. Take time to listen to it, be with it and nourish it. Once you have developed an awareness of your own physical body, you can then explore the outer world without the danger of getting lost.

I love to make pots on a wheel. Moulding clay with my hands and shaping it with the forces of the spinning wheel into beautiful containers fulfils me. To be successful, aside from practice, I have to be centred and grounded. If I take my emotional turmoil into the pottery with me, my pots end up as a sorry mess in the recycling bucket. I see my ability to shape a tall pot as a direct reflection of how I am feeling. When I make a pot I first push the clay down firmly onto the baseboard and centre it. From there I can open it up and raise the clay upwards to form the pot. Failure to prepare the base of the pot properly because I have been too impatient nearly always ends in tears. If we overlook the base chakra in our haste to develop the higher centres we too may end up on the scrap heap.

SELF-ASSESSMENT

Physical Examine your range of movement from the pelvis down. How do your hips, knees and ankles feel? These junctions enable you to move on the earth; they form your support, your roots, your foundation, they carry you. Is there pain, restriction of movement, tightness or inflexibility? How stable do you feel on your legs? Observe your lower back. Is there pain or possibly sciatica? Do you suffer from constipation or irritable bowel syndrome? These are all signs of a lack of Ki being available for the parts of your physical body governed by the base chakra.

Psychological/ Emotional Do you feel abundant, and prosperous, or do you worry about money? Do you think that money is always going out and not coming in? Do you meet survival challenges with optimism and trust or fear and paranoia? Do you find it easy to share what you have or do you hold on to it and hoard? Is the petrol tank of your car always empty or full? Are you always in debt whatever you earn, or do you trust that when you truly need something the money will be there? Do you think the world is just there to be exploited or would you always consider the environmental impact of any investment you made? Do you have a sense of wonder and gratitude to the earth or do you feel disconnected and caught up in your own personal dramas?

EXERCISES

Walking Meditation Within the soles of each foot are minor chakras. Their function is like any major chakra in that they exchange energy with the inner and outer world. The feet are highly sensitive and the following exercise is best done in nature without wearing either shoes or socks.

Walk barefoot on the earth very slowly, each step a moment in time, a conscious connection to earth. Walk on grass, leaves, stones, mud and sand. Walk for a time with your eyes closed exploring with each step the path in front of you.

Administer Reiki to the base of the spine, the hips, knees and feet. Refer to the full treatment.

VISUALISATION

Sit cross-legged on the earth, or stand barefoot with the feet apart. Visualise the planet, a huge sphere slowly rotating through space. Think of her as your mother: your body comes from her and is made of the same elements and matter. Visualise the atmosphere above you, a bubble that surrounds you that regulates your environment, protects you, and creates stability. As the atmosphere is part of the earth, see how you are actually within the earth, in the womb of the earth. Take a breath. The air you are breathing is given to you freely. Meditate on all the nourishment and security the Mother Earth offers you – shelter, water, food, oxygen, light, heat, gravity, stable temperature, power, metals, oils, gems, companions from the animal kingdom, sound, music and so on. Ask yourself if you have ever been without anything you truly needed. Relax and know you are safe.

VISUALISATION

2nd Chakra: Swadhistana

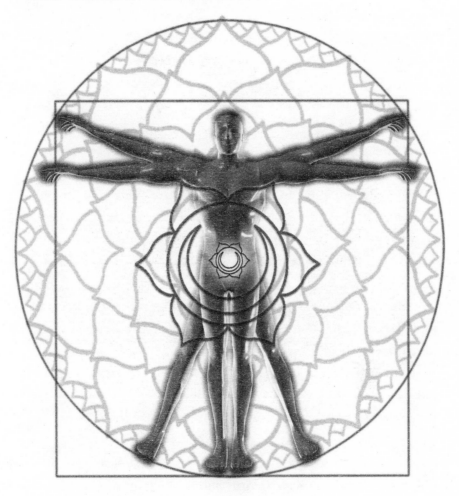

SACRAL CHAKRA

S wadhistana means 'our dwelling place' and this energy centre is often referred to as the sacral chakra, suggesting the 'sacredness' of our own dwelling place. It is situated approximately a hand's width below the belly button and governs the whole pelvic region. The backbone, which forms part of the pelvis, is known as the sacrum. The physical organs governed by this chakra are contained and protected within this sacred space and are primarily concerned with reproduction and excretion. They are the genitals, womb, ovaries, testes, bladder and kidneys.

The element water rules the second chakra. This takes the form of emotional and physical feelings. Energy that has been anchored securely in the solidity and security of the base chakra enters this watery realm and has an opportunity to expand and flow out. The emphasis now is on a sensory exploration of our world rather than a rooting connection to it. This is demonstrated when a child begins to walk for the first time – the point at which the second chakra's development begins, according to Anodea Judith in the book, *Eastern Body, Western Mind.* The child, now able to move independently, follows her own impulses to explore and interact with her environment. I observed this rapid development in my own daughter, at age one year she started to walk. As she began exploring her environment she would always make sure I was there with her. I represented her security and through my support she felt safe to explore her world. She would hold my hand and lead me where she wished to go. When she felt familiarity with her surroundings she would let go of my hand and stride forwards confidently. As soon as she was unsure, she reached up and took hold of my hand again. Slowly her world widened and she learned to trust her own senses. A favourite route for her was to walk around the back of the garage and eat the raspberries from the bushes there. This was a beautiful illustration of second chakra development. She was gaining independence through exploration and she received the sensory reward of finding the berries and tasting them. After a while she only needed me to pick the berries that were out of her reach. Sharing the berries with me was her way of saying, 'Look what I've found! Aren't I clever?' This exploration is an important process for all children, helping them to develop personal confidence in their own senses and providing the impetus to explore further. For a parent it is important to give the space required to the child while being there for him to run back to when he becomes fearful.

Assigned to the second chakra is the Moon and her gentle pull, which so affects our oceans and tides, exercises a similar pull over the watery aspects of the organs contained within the sacral centre. The woman's menstrual cycle is regulated by the 28-day cycle of the moon often referred to as the moon cycle. In the moon's cycle we see her journey from dark to light, representing the duality of nature. The second chakra is the first point of integration between the two serpents of Ida and Pingala that bring energy up from the base chakra. They represent the duality of the human energy system. They leave the base chakra where they are swimming in unity and oneness, separate into the male and female energies and meet once again at the sacral centre in the waters of the moon goddess. The sacredness of the second chakra is symbolised by the function of the womb, offered up to Universal Creation for the conception, protection, nurture and growth of new life. This sacred dwelling place within each of us is a place of personal transformation. Here we give birth metaphorically to our creativity, sensuality, feelings, emotions and physical movement. It is where we conceive, protect, nurture and birth ourselves.

As we begin to develop this chakra, our consciousness, which has known only unity through the first chakra, now experiences duality for the first time. This occurs in the energy channels themselves through the duality of Ida and Pingala and also in the sensory exploration of the outer world. We learn to experience the world through feelings and emotions, and since this world is so rich and full of such experiences we are completely saturated in them. As adults, a potential pitfall for the evolution of consciousness when surrounded by such an abundance of stimuli is that we begin to develop preferences. This creates duality and polarity where previously none existed. We prefer nice, pleasurable and good experiences to ugly, painful and bad. As the second chakra is all about our sensuality and sexuality, it is all too easy to be seduced by what appears nice on the surface but which proves to be ugly when we look deeper. There is nothing wrong with duality, as long as we are willing to embrace the polarities of both bad and good, for then we can begin to integrate them. However, we tend to push the negative away, becoming endless pleasure junkies, constantly pursuing what makes us feel good in the belief it will make us happy, but all the while feeling unsatisfied within. Life then becomes a series of 'I'll be happy if I have that in my life' scenarios – that kind of relationship, that affair, that car, that drink, that job.

The development of the first chakra is to do with stability, grounding and trust. The emphasis in the second chakra is on centring – on developing an energetic, emotional and physical sense of self. By becoming aware of our personal sacred dwelling place we interact with the outside world through grace and harmony rather than need and want. This is vital if we are to develop discernment and constraint when faced with numerous external temptations that promise us everything, but usually only pull us from our centre.

Sexual energy is very potent, it is the creative juice of the Universe; learning to be in it and not abuse it is a large part of second chakra development. The sacral centre is the well from which we draw the effervescence that gives life to all we create. So through the development of this chakra we learn self-control, we learn to contain ourselves and conserve our energy. From here we choose what and whom we allow into our sacred space and to what and to whom we flow out.

I have always thought the suit of cups in the Tarot deck illustrates this very well. Each card shows the various ways water can be contained in a vessel creating positive and negative influences over the contents. Abundance, luxury, spillage, waste, drought and stagnation are all dependent on how the water is held. In much the same way, our vital sensual, sexual and creative energy is affected by how we hold it and the influences that are placed upon it. When not subject to a healthy containment this energy can leak out, stagnate or be wasted.

We experience the meeting of the energies from Pingala and Ida during sexual intimacy. After orgasm there is a feeling of peace and relaxation, this is the result of Ki being released through the body from this storehouse. I first experienced the true potential of this energy on the power point in Scotland. What fired up through me was born in the second chakra. I was prevented from feeling this previously because I was holding separation issues in the third chakra and suppressing energy in the first and second chakras that needed to rise up and transform. The combination of the power point's energy and my new-found tenderness, openness and acceptance of the people around me had created just the right set of circumstances to awaken the sleeping serpent – Kundalini – in the base chakra. As the Kundalini energy moved up through me it caused the 2nd chakra to spin, as the two channels carrying this energy – Ida and Pingala – met. This is what I felt physically. As this energy met in '*my dwelling place*', it caused any blocked energy to transform and gave birth to a new me. Once free to move into the solar plexus, the Ki was able to expand out through my energy channels in one great cosmic orgasm; any toxic energy that I was holding in the lower chakras was cleansed in the fire of the solar plexus.

In July 2000, I attended a seminar in Scotland on earth healing, entitled: *Earth Changes And Human Response* run by Marko Pokajnick, a leading expert on earth energy healing. He took us to the site on Cluny hill, Forres where I had had this experience seven years earlier and explained its function. It is known as Venus hill and is part of a huge landscape temple – Earth Chakra – made up of seven hills arranged in a circle around a basin like valley in the centre. He told us it was one of the main balance points of male and female energy on the planet. As you can imagine, I found that very interesting!

IMBALANCES

The conscious development of the second chakra is to find a sense of self, and to develop our centre as a place from which we merge with the external world, expressing our sensory, emotional, creative and sexual nature. Our objective is to harmonise, contain and centre our dual self within this sacred space, developing healthy personal boundaries.

Imbalance causes us to lose our centre and consequently lose touch with our self. This has a huge effect on our emotional stability, which alters the messages we send out about our personal space. Our boundaries become confusing as others pick up the mixed messages that we send out. We can become overly aggressive, biting people's heads off for no apparent reason, and pushing them away when all we really want is a hug. We can become unreachable, hiding within ourselves, holding all our torment inside and unable to understand why nobody notices we need help. We can allow our personal boundaries to become so weak that we allow others to invade our sacred space and we lose contact with who we are.

Emotional exchange can take place within relationships of all kinds. The intimacy of a sexual relationship is the place where most of us begin to discover what imbalances exist within us. As a sexual relationship calls for an intimate union between two individuals, if the dual selves of the individuals concerned are not integrated and whole, there will be an imbalance in each person before the relationship has even started. The union of the two will then play out those imbalances in conflicts and difficulties as each tries to integrate the other. This is the basis of many personal relationships and it reveals itself in the way most people always want their partner to change to suit them. What would be better is to integrate the good and bad of oneself, the light and the shadow, before even attempting a relationship. As we don't do that, we often find our shadow side expressed through our partner, an extraordinary manifestation of all we are unable to recognise as coming from within.

If we examine the imbalance of the second chakra, there are obvious links to the misuse of sexual energy. Sexual energy is such a powerful force. Unless we are conscious of the strong impulses that can arise from it and develop discernment, there is a danger we may act in ways that cause long-lasting hurt, damage and shame. If people feel a lack of self-worth, this will breed neediness, and they will constantly seek approval and validation. If that neediness is directed sexually, then there is a danger that they will seek out serial sexual partners, trying to find one that will give them what they need. Unfortunately, all they will validate is their own lack of wholeness.

Sexual abuse is an extreme example of sexual misuse, which has deeply destabilising effects on the functioning of the second chakra. Abuse is the most damaging assault on the healthy development of this centre. It creates deep scars that prevent the flow of energy through the rest of the energy system. It will undermine any trust that has been built, strip away any sense of personal boundaries and affect future relationships. I have been astonished at the number of people I have treated with Reiki that have suffered abuse. It has been common for the person to have no recollection of the abuse having taken place; often they have sought treatment because of apparently unrelated issues. Physical problems with the sexual organs, emotional difficulties in relationships, eating disorders, depression, low self-worth and drug problems are just some of the difficulties faced. All these turned out to be secondary issues, the Reiki treatment bringing the cause to the surface – the memory of a sexual abuse. Obviously this was very traumatic for the person, but it demonstrated to me how deeply abuse could be buried by the psyche.

Our present society reflects our polarised natures. We enjoy the guilt, shame and denial of some religions who regard sexual nature as something immoral, dirty and deprived, something that needs to be suppressed or risen above in order to find salvation. And then we open the newspapers and read in great detail about the latest vicar who has fallen from grace after having an affair with one of the congregation. We are taught to suppress emotions, rigidly controlling what is deemed antisocial behaviour. We are presented with a model for decent behaviour that doesn't sit naturally. We live constantly in judgement of all that we suppress within ourselves for fear that it will surface and reveal our own divided and dual nature. We project outwardly on to others what we are unable to accept as coming from within. We model ourselves on one aspect of ourselves, whether light or dark, positive or negative, and become stuck in that polarity.

Monoculture is a catch phrase that describes the expansion and imposition of a single set of values. It incorporates education, history, religion, policing, common culture, TV, music, diet and so on. All wars are fought because of polarity, because nations with opposing beliefs and interests are unwilling to embrace their differences. The sacred dwelling place of each culture is so ingrained by a mono polar set of values, and so quick to judge any differing viewpoint, that they will fight over their right to impose their view.

The Universe itself is complete even though it is dual in nature. We are never separate from creation unless we choose to be so. An imbalance then within this chakra separates us not only from ourselves, but also from our home – Creation itself.

SELF-ASSESSMENT

Physical Do you suffer from lower back pain? If so it is possible your kidneys are not functioning healthily. The kidneys, governed by the second chakra, serve by separating substances not required by the body from those that are. Stress being an emotional toxin affects the healthy functioning of your kidneys. Another area affected by emotional stress or trauma such as abuse, is the sacrum, which can become misaligned, creating a tilt in the pelvis, which in turn leads to mobility problems in the hips. Things to look for in the reproductive organs in men are problems with the prostrate and testicles and general infections and in women are cysts in the ovaries, fibroids in the uterus, an erratic menstruation cycle, pain during intercourse and general infections.

Psychological/Emotional As we have seen above, negative emotions can lead to many problems physically by severing the energy flow to the organs from the governing chakra. Such emotions like guilt and shame can cause depression, sexual frigidity, dependency, feelings of inadequacy, low self-esteem and despair. Emotional imbalance manifests as over- and under-reactions, which are a sign that we have lost our centre. Unresolved anger is better out than in, but if it is directed without awareness at another then it is not constructive to anyone and can cause deep hurt. Developing emotional maturity is learning how to *respond* in conflict situations instead of *react*. By responding from our centre we can help resolve conflicts whilst maintaining our personal boundaries. If we are not centred we either under- or over-react to conflict from an already fragile place, and become defensive or aggressive as we try to enforce our boundaries. This only serves to fuel and escalate the problem.

EXERCISES

Rotation Of The Pelvis Stand with your hands on your pelvis and your legs shoulder-width apart. Slowly move your pelvis to the front and then to the back and then from the left to the right. Finally, make one gentle circular movement, round and round. Try to move just the pelvis, and nothing else.

Meditation On Water Water is the element of the second chakra and relates to inner and outer purification.

MEDITATION ON WATER

For an inner purification exercise, take a cool glass of water and, while sitting, drink it slowly. Feel the passage of water as it flows through you. Feel the freshness in your mouth, throat, stomach and abdomen. Imagine it is clearing away all impurities and when you go to the bathroom, let them go.

For an outer purification exercise, take a shower in cool water, or better still, bathe in a river or waterfall. As the water flows over your body let it take away your negative feelings and thoughts. Say to yourself, "Now my body is clean. Now my feelings are clean. Now my mind is clean."

3rd Chakra: Manipura

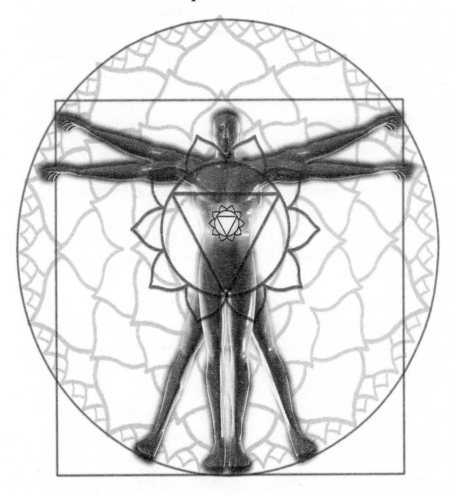

SOLAR PLEXUS CHAKRA

C ommonly known as the power centre, this chakra is found at the solar plexus, just below the sternum. Ruled by the element of fire, this centre is the furnace that purifies toxicity on all levels within the surface bodies. Manipura means 'the place of jewels'. In alchemy, fire is the element into which base metals are placed in order to turn them to gold. In the same way, the place of jewels is the body's alchemical fire that burns away all impurity and leaves only the purity of the golden self. This chakra governs our power and will and so the solar plexus is where the elements of the lower chakras, earth and water, are brought to create wilful action. From here we are energised by the heat of fire, which gives life to our bodies, our inner passions and provides the fuel for us to achieve through action. The solar plexus gives strength and vitality to our energy field; it is the power that declares, "I am here!"

Physically, the solar plexus corresponds to the coeliac plexus, a network of nerves that meet here. These connect to the stomach, pancreas, liver, gall bladder and spleen, the organs that are primarily concerned with digestion, detoxification and sugar regulation. The stomach is literally like an acid bath, breaking down and digesting foods with incredible efficiency. The liver detoxifies our blood, the gall bladder secretes bile into the duodenum to neutralise the acids from the stomach. The pancreas controls sugar levels and the spleen the production of white blood cells, the storage of blood and the final destruction of old blood cells. This area of the body is linked to expressions such as "I can't stomach this!" suggesting someone who has had enough of a situation. "To vent one's spleen", is another saying which describes the expression of frustration or anger. These are uncannily accurate characteristics of the third chakra.

As power and personal will are the themes of this chakra, whenever we experience conflict, this is where it is felt. Sitting above the second chakra, which governs our sense of self worth and emotional balance, this centre is affected by any imbalances that rise up. Any deficiencies in this chakra will affect our vitality and personal strength and will be discernible from the outside. Polarised issues begin to emerge – strength versus weakness, dominance versus submission, winner versus loser. This misunderstanding of the nature of true power sets up the misuse of power. The energetic communication between people becomes one of trying to constantly gain the upper hand and any intuitive gifts are directed towards probing the opposition for weaknesses. These are old polarised views of power. We need to learn to be powerful without dis-empowering others.

Being related to power and will, this chakra is the home of the ego – and it won't like me giving it a little E! This is the personalised consciousness that makes its way in the world. From here we develop our own personal truth. We have the possibility to be unique and develop in ways that define the self. To be unique means to sometimes swim against the tide, to risk criticism and torment. If this is our truth then the power from this chakra will give us the strength to persist.

In this chakra the process of individuation really begins. This is symbolised by breaking away from the control, influence and beliefs of external sources. It is the symbolic cutting of the umbilical cord from our mothers. In the book *Iron John* by Robert Bly, the teenage boy has to steal the golden key from under the pillow of his mother to free the wild man from the courtyard prison. The wild man is a symbol of his own rebellious self and he has to steal the key because his mother will never give it to him freely. By cutting the umbilical cord we make a statement: "I am able to think, feel, act and survive by myself! I am my own authority. I no longer need a hand to hold!" This process in traditional chakra theory takes place between 14 and 21 years of age. The rebellious nature of teenagers is their way of establishing personal power and individuality. In her book *Eastern Medicine, Western Mind* Anodea Judith places this chakra's development between the ages of 2 and 4 years old. This is the onset of the infamous terrible twos and is a demonstration of the child's will rebelling in order to establish independence.

The alternative is to comply with popular opinion because it takes less energy and requires no strength. The result is a weakening of the individual spirit and the loss of freedom. Imbalance in the lower two chakras will prevent the individuation process through lack of trust and self-worth. If we are emotionally insecure and untrusting of our place in the world, then it is virtually impossible to develop a sense of personal power that does not depend on the domination of another. The development of an ego self is an important part of our ability to function in this world, but if the ego uses its power over others, if it sees itself as separate from others, it immediately polarises itself and the world and the people in it become something that the ego needs to defend itself and protect itself from.

The ego is healthy if it is in a state of surrender to Creation and open to the influence of energy coming down through the heart from the higher chakras. The solar plexus then becomes the meeting place of Universal love and creation and the personalised self that has risen through the development of the first and second chakras. The energy of the solar plexus, the force behind action, then becomes the vehicle through which Truth, Love and personal expression are given life outwardly. If the ego disregards the Universal love flowing from the heart and has an imbalance in the energy arriving from the lower chakras, it will suffer distortion.

Power, which the ego holds, manifests itself through the ego's role of being the decision maker. The ego has the power to choose. If the ego chooses to believe in an illusory reality, it has the power to not only do so, but also continue to use its power to further create the illusion. This in turn validates its beliefs. Any time something touches the ego, which could threaten its view of reality, the ego will quickly move to defend itself.

As the development of the third chakra is to do with the formation of personal authority and the integration of power, imbalances in this centre can occur when our power is given over to an outside authority. The formation of the individual self expressed through the ego takes place in childhood. The boundaries placed on the child in the form of manners, rules and discipline are supposed to help the child develop correct conduct. They determine what is acceptable social behaviour within the child's environment. When boundaries are confusing and keep shifting, the developing child loses trust in the authority. If these boundaries are enforced inconsistently, sometimes aggressively, sometimes tentatively, the child becomes fearful and unsure how to act. The inner authority of the child takes its cue from the external authority and develops boundaries of similar confusion. The active will of the child will then develop either aggressive or submissive behaviour, because that's how it has been taught.

Instead of an authority teaching the child healthy boundaries, how to think for itself and develop its own will, the distorted authority will inadvertently destabilise the child's will and create insecurity. The result will be negative emotional disturbances within the power centre. Feelings of shame can arise through excessive judgement and criticism or through having to conform against their wishes. This is the origin of the phrase "to have power over someone". This so called disciplining of children is really to do with controlling their wilful nature, often using punishment to enforce the rules. There is a big difference between establishing healthy boundaries and the enforced control of rules through intimidation. Most children are highly perceptive and soon see when an authority is saying "do what I say not what I do". Being a conformist has its rewards but at the expense of individuality. Our wilful nature gets angered when suppressed and if it only has distortion on which to model itself, then what is learned is the use of power in unhealthy ways; the manipulation of power in order to achieve or get what we want originates here.

In adulthood, a lack of personal authority manifests itself in a search for approval from an outside authority. Our sense of power becomes dependent on outside acceptance and our sense of pride is gained through approval and recognition from a power source we don't control. We begin to define ourselves by the approval or lack of it that we receive through our actions. If we perform well at work and it is recognised, we get praise and we feel powerful; if not and we are criticised, we feel weak.

Highly sensitive people often find it difficult to be in this world because they feel overwhelmed by the dominant behaviour of others. Anger, aggression, competitiveness, and controlling behaviour may remind them of an overbearing parent or teacher. Many people who practice Reiki or similar disciplines suddenly find themselves susceptible to such energies as their own defensive layer is stripped away. Many protective techniques have been developed to deal with this issue, but it indicates that they are experiencing such feelings externally because they suppressed similar feelings long ago. Looking within will often reveal that we have not healed the lower chakras and have still to find inner balance. We are still operating on the principle of preference. Even though we may like to believe we are open and at one with everything, as soon as something comes along that doesn't feel good to us we move to defend and protect ourselves.

IMBALANCES

Ailments occurring as a result of a dysfunction in this chakra can affect all the organs governed by it. we find various digestive problems here which include, hiatus hernias, ulcers, loss of appetite and bulimia . Someone I know suffering with bulimia for many years told me when she made herself sick, it was to throw up the things she was unable to stomach. She is very open and feels external emotions and conflict acutely. Her bulimia was her way of getting rid of them. The healthy functioning of the liver, pancreas and spleen are all affected by suppressed and unexpressed anger leading to a range of ailments. Our skeletal structure can also suffer with upper back and neck problems leading to headaches and migraines. These have their roots in the spine losing it's alignment by the person repeatedly moving into defence postures. Problems in the shoulders and neck can be due to carrying the weight of expectations and the burdens of shame. Often a signal that we have lost the power to live our own independent lives free of emotional manipulation. Eating disorders, digestive problems and ulcers due to not being able to stomach conflicts and power struggles. Diabetes and hypoglycaemia not being able to control our own metabolism. Diseases in the liver and spleen from the anger of being controlled and manipulated.

An afflicted solar plexus chakra will result in difficulty in managing power. Either the power centre will be over-active resulting in aggressive, dominating, controlling, manipulative, violent, sadistic, stubborn or arrogant behaviour and short tempers. Or alternatively, it will be under-active displaying weakness, despair, hopelessness, pessimism, masochism, victim mentality and unreliability.

Nowhere else is that popular expression in the new age, Dis-Ease more appropriate than here in the third chakra.

SELF-ASSESSMENT

Physical It is difficult to separate the physical, emotional and psychological issues of the power centre because an ailment in one is very clearly connected to the other. For the purpose of assessing yourself and others, a useful tool is to examine body posture and language. To diagnose an imbalance in the solar plexus look at the way a person holds themselves, because the body doesn't lie. Folding the arms across the solar plexus is a posture that expresses inner anxiety and is the most commonly seen form of defence. When a person feels exposed or emotionally vulnerable they will fold their arms low across the stomach, bending forwards in a submissive posture. An aggressive stance is similar but the arms will cross slightly higher and the body will lean back, pushing the chest out. The postures are both unconscious physical reactions that reflect the anxiety felt in the power centre to potential conflict. Suffering from any of the physical disorders mentioned will be an indication of energy imbalance in this centre.

Psychological/Emotional   Anger directed inward causes great toxicity to the digestive organs and to their healthy functioning, and if directed outward inflicts that same toxicity on someone else. If the solar plexus is imbalanced in a person there may be a lack of fire and therefore vitality, they may give their personal power away to another. They may be highly anxious, retiring or shy. Such a person will appear weak with a pessimistic attitude. If the fire is overly present, a person may be aggressive, controlling, egocentric and generally insensitive. They may be prone to dominate others and have a sadistic streak in them.

EXERCISES

How often have you caught yourself making harsh judgements of people and situations around you? Part of the process of living in a world of rigid beliefs and opinions is the need to constantly validate them. The way in which we do that is to project our ideology on to the world. If people do not conform to our views we find ourselves judging them. We become intolerant and prejudiced. If we were to turn the judgements around and bring them back to ourselves we would see how harsh and arrogant they are. Below is an exercise to help in the acceptance of the world and the people around you.

Breathing In Judgements, Breathing Out Acceptance
Marko Pokajnick
Begin by simply sitting and looking at the situation that you find yourself at issue with.

As you breathe in, take back all judgements you have made. As you breathe out, exhale acceptance of the situation as is. Repeat the process until you feel a sense of gratitude within yourself. This exercise can be done with another person and is particularly useful with a partner.

The Fist Form a fist with one of your hands. Imagine this fist is your solar plexus. Visualise the holding, the tightness. What does a clenched fist represent to you? Is it anger, fighting, holding, aggression, defence, rage or protection?

Now unclench your fist, let it become relaxed and open palmed. How would your solar plexus feel if it was like this? Visualise the relaxation, the release, the openness and welcome of an open hand. Imagine being with people like this.

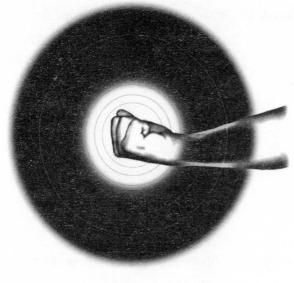

HAND CLENCHED

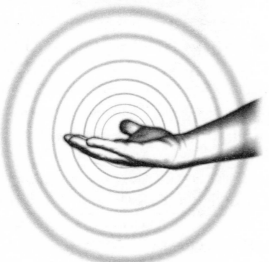

PALM OPEN

4th Chakra: Anahata

HEART CHAKRA

Also known as the heart centre, this chakra is situated in the middle of the chest and provides vital energy to the physical heart and lungs. Anahata means 'That which is ever new', suggesting that the essence of the heart chakra is perpetual newness, an ever-filling cup of love. It is assigned the colour emerald green, which is found in the centre of the rainbow. Our intimate connection to the earth is felt through the heart. The green of nature resonates with the colour of this centre and nurtures the heart. Governed by the element air, from here humans exchange breath with their surroundings in the same way the great forests act as the lungs of the earth. The openness of this centre dictates the intimacy we have with our environment. A singer cannot sing without breath and cannot sing sweetly without love.

The heart centre is the centre of our energy system. Symbolised by the upright and inverted triangles, which decree as above, so below. The heart centre is our true resting place, where the flow of energies from the spirit self and the earth self meet. The heart is where we can see what is presently flowing through someone. If the flow of energy coming from the lower chakras and higher chakras bears hurt, grudges, betrayal or abandonment and the mind is dwelling on them and perpetuating them, then that is what will be expressed through the heart. It is said the eyes are the 'mirrors to the soul' and the soul resides within the heart. Is it any wonder a child's eyes look right through you, wide open, nothing to hide and so very bright? They are simply reflecting the openness of their hearts. If the heart hardens and moves to protect itself, that too will be reflected in the eyes. To be, is to dwell within the heart regardless of what is taking place around us. Being unconditionally open is probably the most difficult step for us to take in order to become a human being.

The heart centre pulls us into bonds with others, it is from this centre that we form deep friendships and intimate relationships. In a perfect world, the love we feel for another would remain even in the midst of conflict. It would not depend on the other person giving us what we want. How our partner behaved or responded to us would be of no relevance, our love would remain without conditions. But how we love and the openness of our heart becomes dependent on how we have evolved through the lower centres. If, during our emotional development, we were abandoned or hurt in some way we will carry that as fractures within. The issues we now carry can undermine any relationship we may form. A lack of trust, a lack of emotional security, a lack of self-worth, and a lack of personal authority when brought into personal relationships do not exactly make for a harmonious union. We place conditions on our present relationships because of being hurt in the past. Our heart opens and closes depending on how our partner acts towards us. If our needs are met we open up our hearts and love. If not, we close off and reject our partners, withdrawing our love. A relationship has the potential to show us where our issues lie. Through the dynamics and dramas of our present relationships our past shadows reveal themselves. If the relationship is secure, it provides a healthy place for us to integrate those long suppressed aspects.

A true relationship is found through the intimacy of the heart. If two partners exist together from this centre and issues arise from the lower centres creating conflict, the partners will in time learn it is never worth withdrawing their love and closing their hearts to each other. It is far better to trust the heart than the patterns of conflict that arise. If we move successively from relationship to relationship it is because we crave the pleasure that intimacy brings but don't embrace the pain. When issues rise up to be examined from our ego self and manifest as conflict, we recoil. Feeling hurt and angry we separate and look for someone else to feel pleasure with once more, but the same conflicts will always arise in the new partner.

To be in love is to see with childlike eyes again; love pierces the heart with warmth and its soft petals open like a delicate flower on a sunny day. The loss of love causes the personalised self, the ego, to retreat back to where it came from, back to the lower chakras, to the issues and patterns. Here it seeks to justify never having to open up again, it sides with its imbalances, and its shadow says, "See I told you it's unsafe to love, far better to never open, stay down here with me." The day that love is lost from the outside and instead of retreating we remain in our heart, allow the pain in and stay open to it to the same degree as we were to the pleasure of love, is the day we anchor ourselves in the heart. Once we have experienced an open heart we will always yearn to feel it again. We know it is how we are meant to be.

So how do we tell if our hearts are open? With an open heart our whole body becomes infused with openness. Our posture will be open, our eyes bright and able to hold a gaze with nothing to hide, our voice will soften and our energy field will radiate warmth and compassion. There will be a very obvious presence, a mix of power and humility. An open heart is a fertile bed that allows our true nature to emerge and reveal itself. Our inner being, higher self, spirit or divine nature speaks from the heart. With an open heart our bodies become infused with love, light and truth. As those qualities fill the mind they bring clarity and our thoughts become loving and truthful. As they fill the emotions we will have true feelings, and as they fill the intuition we will have true perception. If the heart is closed, we can no longer trust what we think, feel or perceive.

It is no surprise to me that Reiki is so popular. In order to channel love the heart simply has to be open. To be in a Reiki workshop is to bathe in the energies of the heart. That openness when experienced is transforming. It helps us to see our shadows from a loving space. It helps us to heal wounds by bringing them into the intimacy of the heart. Viewed from the heart our wounds are seen as something that have always caused separation and hurt. We begin to understand the pain we have caused by acting from our shadow without owning it. Compassion, acceptance and forgiveness for both others and ourselves are found in the gentleness of this chakra.

All healing occurs by bringing whatever the issue is into the heart. Within the heart an issue can be seen for what it really is. It will no longer have such a hold over you, because now being within your heart is matching its attraction with the gentle pull of love. To hold on to the issue would mean to leave the heart and it's never worth it. Compassion, forgiveness, acceptance and wisdom are all qualities developed through the simple act of being in the heart. The heart, with its element of air, gives great freedom to the personal self; the influence of spirit inspiring and uplifting the security-bound self.

In Peter Brooks epic tale *The Mahabarata* there is a scene where the brothers all drink from the poisonous lake and die. The remaining brother finds them dead and pleads with the lake to bring them back to life. The lake says: *"If you answer this question correctly I will, if not you too will die."* The lake then asks, *"What is the most endearing quality of man?"* The brother replies, *"That though he is merely mortal, he lives as if he is eternal."* The lake, satisfied, brings the brothers back to life.

The heart gives us our spirit and courage. We say of a person with courage, "They have the heart of a lion". It is here in the Anahata chakra, '*the timeless jewel for which everything is ever new*', we meet our eternal self.

IMBALANCES

The element air, which governs the heart centre, gives us a clue to how imbalances affect this chakra. The lungs, through the breathing reflex, govern the flow of this element in and out of our body. We all know we cannot continuously breathe out, we would soon turn blue and pass out. If we were to continuously breathe in, we would burst. In the same way, the heart centre enables us to develop the nature of giving and receiving. If we have misunderstood this feature, our tendency will be to give constantly of our love to the detriment of ourselves, or we will never be able to satisfy our longing for love as we constantly look for it from outside ourselves.

To give something, whether it is love, healing, support, advice or gifts must have no personal conditions placed on it. If we keep a record of what it is we have given, only to use it at a later date to manipulate a situation to our advantage, were we really ever giving? If we give to a charity and then tell everyone to demonstrate to others what a caring person we are, who is profiting from the giving? As a therapist, when people come to us for healing, if our sense of self-worth is governed by the successful outcome of the healing, will we push them to emotional releases when it is inappropriate? The wounded healer is a dangerous role to play if we have not fully explored our own wounds, and if we get a sense of wholeness by facilitating others in their personal process to go into places we have not been prepared to go ourselves.

By constantly giving we stay in control and smother and deny people the space to nurture themselves. They need to eat when they want to, heal when they want to, share when they want to and to release when they want to. So to give, we must examine our true motives and be careful we are not gaining more from the act of giving than the person we are giving to.

Receiving requires us to be like an open receptacle into which a giver can pour their gifts. So often we fail to receive gracefully. It is as if we feel we don't deserve to receive, we are unworthy. More often than not, people are more comfortable giving than receiving. It is important to realise that when we receive we do so with love. To maintain the integrity of an exchange, both elements need to be in place. This is why it is sometimes difficult to help people who do not believe they are deserving of good fortune; they simply cannot receive.

In relationships, this process of giving and receiving is distorted frequently. We offer love if our partners act in appropriate ways. When things are to our liking we love, as soon as things are not to our liking we withdraw our love. Co-dependency is where we become obsessed with our partner, unable to function healthily within the relationship and unable to function without it. We can be possessive, jealous and place all kinds of conditions on our partners. Love is our greatest addiction and as with any addiction we lose sight of what is good for us and will often get pulled into abusive relationships that reflect our wounded selves. Patterns form in relationships that reflect the imbalance of energy in the heart centre. We fall in love projecting absolute perfection on our partners and a few months later coldly withdraw and reject the same person, declaring "They were not like that when I met them."

So our heart chakra reveals its imbalances either through excessive acts of love outwards that only serve to satisfy ourselves, or by shutting off and withdrawing into the self and coldly rejecting love from within our shell.

The only thing really worth anything is the integration of consciousness within an open heart. To close it is to deny Creation the very dwelling place it created you for. To have a closed heart is to never know this eternal self. It is to cling to the earth, be tossed in the emotional waters and fight in the fires of conflict. Only through the heart can we rise up from who we think we are to become what we really are – a human being.

SELF-ASSESSMENT

Physical When the heart is closed off, the body language becomes stiff and rigid. If such a person is held in an embrace, they are unable to soften. The closed heart reveals a wounded interior. It reveals a person who feels unloved and unlovable and who is unwilling to risk being loved for fear of being hurt again.

When the heart is open and the energy of giving is the main focus, the person will have open body language. They will always wish to hug you, listen to you or know what's going on. Their embraces will feel suffocating, as if they are taking more than they are giving.

Problems with respiration, like asthma, bronchitis and general shallow breathing indicate heart chakra imbalance. Depression and heart problems may also manifest themselves.

Psychological/Emotional Idealistic and over-romanticised ideas of love, conditional love, obsessive, jealous, possessive and smothering love are all indicative of an emotional or psychological imbalance in this chakra. When someone gives you something you say, "Oh no, I couldn't possibly accept that!"

Conversely, pessimism, bitterness, cruelty, anger, isolation, loneliness and obnoxious behaviour that purposely pushes people away can manifest as imbalances in this chakra.

EXERCISES

Marko Pokajnick

The central symbol within the heart chakra is the Star of David, the upright and inverted triangles that symbolise as above, then so below. In this exercise we create this symbol with the arms and declare our connection to both earth and spirit.

Stand with your feet shoulder width apart and knees slightly bent. Form a V-angle with your hands pointing downwards, palms inwards, fingers touching at the base chakra. Draw your arms upwards to form an imaginary inverted triangle and outwards till fully extended above your head. State in your mind Earth to Spirit. Then bring your fingers together palms facing each other above your head and draw an imaginary triangle downwards and outwards stating Spirit to Earth. Repeat the exercise until you feel you are truly connected.

Breathe As the element of this chakra is air, by focusing on the heart centre and breathing consciously into it, we can help it to open. This is a good exercise to do anytime, but particularly good before giving healing.

5th Chakra: Vishuddha

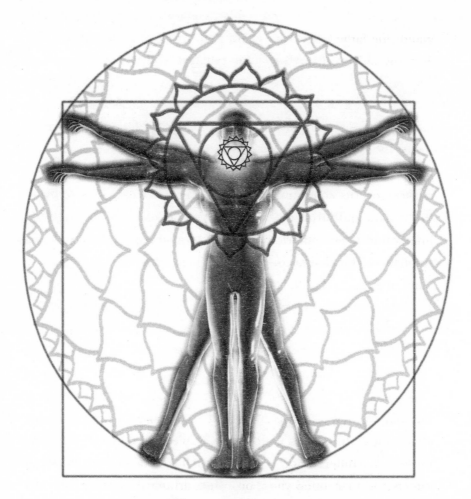

THROAT CHAKRA

C ommonly known as the throat chakra, as its name suggests, it is situated in the throat region and corresponds to the thyroid gland, the large endocrine gland that lies at the base of the neck. The thyroid produces hormones that affect cellular metabolism, stimulate the growth and development of the physical body, encourage the onset of puberty and the development of sexual maturity. Situated around the fourth cervical vertebra it governs the larynx, ears and mouth. The Vishuddha chakra is the bridge between our inner self and outer creation. Situated at the throat, this chakra governs communication. The element ether is assigned to this chakra and forms the basis for the many layers of existence to interconnect. The etheric realm is that of vibration, frequency and resonance. This chakra connects us to all layers of Creation, physical, emotional, mental, will, intuition and spirit, by way of vibration.

When we talk our speech is literally made up of vibrations that impact on the eardrum of the listener. These are translated into recognisable sounds and interpreted by the mind as words. If you place a speaker playing loud music next to a glass of water, the water will resonate with the sound vibrations, displaying the frequencies of the sound as ripples on its surface. What is more interesting are the effects music has on us emotionally. A piece of classical music will move us in a different way to heavy rock. It is through this that we can understand that sound vibrations when arranged together carry the composer's intention to the listener. If the music is melancholic, it will provoke a melancholic response, if joyful, it will provoke a happy one.

In the same way, our voice communicates not only our words but also the emotional charge behind them. A teacher enthusiastic about his subject conveys that enthusiasm to his students. If we are joyful, that joy will be present in anything we say. So whatever our present condition is, when we express ourselves that too is communicated.

Vibrations are the basic ingredients of Creation. The Big Bang theory, a term coined by physicist George Gamow, suggests that the universe began from the explosion of a single subatomic particle fifteen billion years ago. A radio receiver can still register the fallout from this explosion as a background hum. When you switch on a TV without tuning it to anything you see thousands of dots – you are looking at the same background hum. In the first chapter of the gospel of St John it is written: "In the beginning was the Word and the Word was with God and the Word was God."

Creation is made up of particles that are organised by vibrating at different frequencies. Everything in Creation, from the movement of atoms and electrons to the formation of stars and galaxies, is determined by the frequency at which their composite parts vibrate. Water is a liquid because it vibrates at a particular frequency. Heat it up and the water particles change frequency, speeding up to become a gas. Cool it down and the opposite happens, the particles slow down and the water becomes a solid. So everything is represented by a frequency.

White light when dispersed into its composite parts is made up of seven colours, seven frequencies. These make up the visual spectrum, but there are literally millions of frequencies that we cannot see. The fifth chakra is the centre that determines our spectrum of communication. If it is open and developed we have a far broader spectrum of communication; if it is closed the spectrum is limited.

The emotional and psychological harmony that exists within a person affects their communication. When we are harmonious we resonate in harmony with people and our surroundings. There is an ease, a flow in our interactions that reflects how we feel within. If however, we carry emotional and psychological disharmony within, invariably our relationships to people and our environment will reflect that.

As we have established, the universe is made up of vibrations. If it were possible to hear those vibrations, what would they sound like? Imagine being able to hear the harmony of the universe, an incredible thought. As individuals creating our own song so to speak, we are either in tune or out of tune with the universal song. How do we experience that?

A tennis player experiences harmony as being 'in the zone', where every shot hits its target. A racing driver travelling at 200mph experiences it as if time slows down and things are happening in slow motion. An actor experiences it as if their body is given over to the character they are playing. A Reiki healer experiences it in a similar way, as being a channel. So when we are empty of internal conflict and in harmony within, we resonate with universal harmony and our actions and expressions are in keeping with universal truth.

Part of the function of the fifth chakra is to develop communication on a subtle level. Our etheric bodies are highly sensitive to the energetic emissions around us. Though often unconscious, this subtle communication shapes our interactions and will often prompt a physical response in the form of body language. If someone is projecting anger from the solar plexus for example, it is not uncommon to see people folding their arms to protect themselves. This subtle communication takes place constantly and can be enhanced by cleansing ourselves of emotional, mental and physical toxicity.

Intuitive communication takes place on a vibratory level. The finer our sensitivity, the subtler the vibrations we can communicate with. Guides, angels and elemental beings all communicate through vibration. If we learn to listen we may understand their language.

In the summer of 2000 whilst working with Marko Pokajnik, who I mentioned earlier on the Earth healing and human response workshop, I experienced really sore throats. I was baffled and when I talked to him about it, he smiled and said, "Well you're trying to communicate with earth angels and elemental beings. Your throat centre is opening to new forms of communication, that's why it's hurting." Pretty obvious really but I hadn't even considered it before.

Our ability to communicate is determined by our ability to tune into the frequencies of whatever it is we wish to communicate with, much like a radio receiver being able to pick up different radio stations when tuned to their frequency. If we wish to feel a crystal, we need only hold it and allow ourselves to merge with it. Each crystal will have a frequency and as you and I are part of the same universe we can feel it if we want to. We can feel the emissions from mobile phones – they make our ears hot. Writing this book I can feel my laptop processor emitting a frequency from under the keyboard. We feel the vibe of a place or a person. This is communication and it occurs through the openness of your throat centre.

Each chakra is assigned a frequency of light and sound. The chakras as a whole resonate together to form a harmonious tune, which is you. If a chakra is out of balance we can say it is no longer vibrating at its optimum frequency. If someone in a choir is singing flat, the whole performance is compromised, and, similarly, if one chakra is out of tune it will affect the harmony of all the chakras. Disease is a consequence of our energetic system being disharmonious.

As well as the throat chakra forming a gateway to the outer world, two other important connections are made through this centre. Firstly, the throat centre and the sacral centre are interlinked with each other; there is a recognised energetic connection between them. In Reiki it is common to balance the two chakras by placing a hand over each simultaneously. The sacral chakra contains the creative juice of the energy system and the throat gives expression to it. Consequently, an imbalance in the sacral will create blockages in the throat and vice versa. For example, low self-worth in the sacral chakra causes an inability to express oneself confidently in the throat.

Secondly, the throat centre is the gateway between the heart and mind. The throat is literally a bottleneck through which energy has to pass, and blockages can occur if there is a knowing within the heart that is not accepted by the mind. Often after a Reiki initiation this occurs as people feel the deep connection in the heart but the rational mind won't accept it. The resultant blockage in the throat causes headaches and pain in the C7 joint of the spine. When the energy of the heart is allowed to move up through the throat, we are able to express and speak our truth. Truth is a vibration of the universe. To express truth is to be in harmony with the universe.

If the ingredient of Creation is sound, we can begin to see how Reiki works. Rei Ki is Creation/Energy which is Vibration/Energy. Hands-on healing is often referred to as vibrational healing. An individual's health is relative to the harmonious relationship between the inner alignment of the chakras and the outside world. Disease occurs when there is disharmony anywhere in that relationship. Reiki – the Vibrational Energy of Creation – when given, re-introduces the tone of Creation. We translate that as love or warmth. So in the same way that one would use a tone to balance an individual chakra, in order to balance the whole person we must introduce a tone that reflects Universal harmony – one such tone is Reiki.

IMBALANCES

Whenever we speak, our words are accompanied by intention. If what we express comes from an emotionally balanced or rational place within us, then the listener experiences us as balanced or rational. If our words are intended to manipulate and deceive, then they will carry the energy of deception. If the expression comes from hurt or anger then the energy that accompanies our words will carry that hurt and anger to the listener.

When a person is verbally assaulted, and by that I mean criticised, shouted at, blamed, ridiculed or reproached, the effects on their energetic body are no different to the effects of an assault on the physical body. The assault leaves a trauma or scar. The victim of such an attack will hold all that negative energy within his energetic structure. This creates discord, which is the antithesis to a healthy energetic body. If the ensuing anger and hurt that arises as a result of such an assault fails to find an outlet, its resonance will disrupt their own internal harmony, causing illness.

But what are we supposed to do with trauma? Give it back and risk further assault? Give it to someone else? Or simply carry on holding it within?

This form of conflict is prevalent throughout our society. If we carry unresolved power, control or emotional issues then our interactions with others are going to reflect them. Even if we profess to be developed and conscious, there will always be fields of energy with which we don't resonate.

Vishuddha means 'purest of the pure', so part of the fifth chakra development is to purify the self. This process requires us to accept that our interaction with the external world will only be as harmonious as we are within. From this perspective, conflicts that arise in our lives are reflections of inner conflicts. Through examining our external conflicts we can see what is not harmonious within.

I was once told a story of a man who was deeply in love with a woman. Because of many arguments they separated and the man married and had a child with someone else. He never stopped loving his first love and though he tried hard to be with his family it was not his truth. In his early 30s he suffered a heart attack. He survived and began to live a double life, meeting his first love secretly. After 17 years of marriage he started to get sore throats and his voice became strained. He was diagnosed with throat cancer, which eventually spread to his brain creating mood swings and confusion. Finally, on the brink of leaving his wife, he died from a second heart attack.

This is a sad story indeed, but an interesting one. The three areas of his body affected by the internal conflict his predicament in the outside world had created were his heart, throat and mind. As we have learned, through the throat chakra we express our inner truth and form a bridge between our hearts and minds. From this centre, 'the purest of the pure', our emotions are given expression.

SELF-ASSESSMENT

Physical Do you suffer from sore throats? Does your voice lack strength? Have you lost your voice? Do you cough a lot to clear your throat, get things stuck in your throat or get a frog in your throat? Do you find it difficult to swallow? Do you stutter? Do you suffer from mouth ulcers, teeth and gum problems, regular stiffness in the neck or headaches? Do you have a lot of accidents, or feel clumsy and out of sync with your surroundings? Do you have rhythm?

Psychological/Emotional Can you express your emotions and opinions clearly? Are you open, and are you willing to hear alternate possibilities? Do you listen in general or find it difficult to concentrate? Do you find people don't listen to you? Do you find people criticise you or get angry towards you a lot? Are you able to respond or do you fall silent? Do you express your creativity? Are you intuitive, psychic or feel things?

EXERCISES

Head Rotation Rotate the head on the shoulders slowly with a circular movement. When you feel tightness or pain, stop and massage the area with your fingers, then resume rotation. Make sure you rotate the head in both directions an equal number of times.

HEAD ROTATION

Expressing In Tones   Toning is a recognised way to harmonise energy; expressing tones on an individual basis is a way of giving expression to your feelings. Find a solitary place in nature and simply allow the tones you make reflect how you feel. If you feel awful make awful tones, if you feel angry or hurt make angry and hurt tones. Slowly you will find the tones will change and become more harmonious. My experience of doing this is that the negative restless energy I feel is replaced by a positive sense of peace. My favourite place to do this is in the sauna. A sauna is a place of purification and what better environment is there to purify the throat, centre of purification. This exercise can be done either as a group or alone.

6th Chakra: Ajna

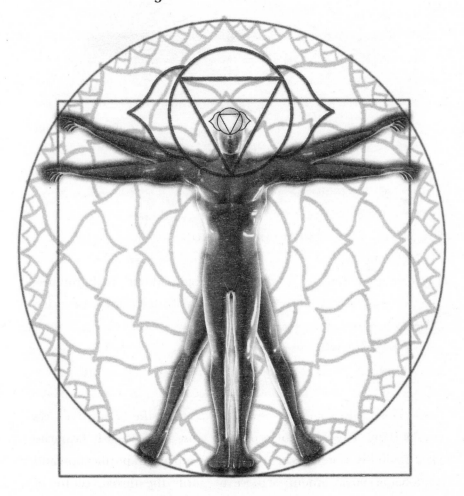

THIRD EYE CHAKRA

"It is better to light a single candle than curse the darkness".

The sixth chakra is found in between the eyebrows and governs the pineal gland in the centre of the head. The element of this chakra is light, which explains its association with inner vision. It is more commonly known as the third eye, the mystical all-seeing eye of wisdom. It is here that the three energy channels Ida, Pingala and Sushumna meet. These three channels started their journey together in the Muladhara chakra. Ida and Pingala intersect each other at each chakra but only meet the central channel again here at the Ajna chakra. So it is here that the energies of duality – the male and female, the sun and moon, the light and dark – finally merge into one in the all seeing eye of wisdom and ascend the Sushumna channel to the final chakra, the crown, to be a fully integrated consciousness.

This image shows us that the purpose of the Ajna chakra, which means command, is to integrate our inner and outer experiences and bring understanding to both by shining light on them, the light of wisdom. To become aware and conscious of what we are, we need to be able to pay attention and focus our mind's eye inwards to observe ourselves.

So the third eye is a vehicle for self-reflection and self-knowledge. From here we establish a command post from which we have an overview. We can observe our internal patterns and monitor our feelings and at the same time see how our behaviour impacts on the outside world. So we could say the ability to become objective and conscious about ourselves originates here. The duality of the sixth chakra is defined by conscious and unconscious existence. We operate consciously when we are aware of our actions. We tend towards mindfulness, temperance, and responsiveness in our interactions. Unconscious behaviour on the other hand, is reactionary, automatic and careless. As humans our unconscious behaviour is often a reflection of our programming. It is our 'default' setting, our pre-programmed reaction to a set of circumstances. By becoming conscious we learn to modify and make adjustments to our behaviour and override our defaults. Our life is and has always been exactly how we have created it. We are never in the wrong place. If we want to change our future, we need to first understand and then take responsibility for the fact we created the past and present. This is the beginning of wisdom.

Intuition is a key function of the sixth chakra. It is the feminine nature of mind. It operates through openness and receptivity. Intuition takes the form of symbolic images that flash across our mind. The third eye is like an internal viewing screen, upon which our intuitions are projected. An intuition is recognisable in that it is accompanied by a deep sense of knowing. Without that, whatever is flashed across the internal viewing screen, in my opinion, cannot be trusted. These intuitions come to us in the form of dreams, visions, telepathy and clairvoyance.

Clairvoyance or clear-seeing is the ability to translate subtle energy from its patterns of vibration into images. When we are receptive to seeing the non-physical it is possible to see the energetic impressions it makes. Seeing auras is seeing the colour frequencies that make up a person's energy field. Seeing guides, angels, ghosts or little green men is a result of this inner eye being tuned in and focused to see those vibrations.

Dreams as intuitions are the symbolic messages that our subconscious mind sends us when the rational mind is asleep. Sometimes we find solutions to our problems through such messages. Other times it is as if we are simply remembering our own true expansive nature. Liberated from the constraints of the physical body, we are able to fly and journey as consciousness in the symbolic realms of the universal mind.

Telepathy is thought communication. Our thoughts are projected into the world as vibrations in the same way as our voice. The frequency of those vibrations is just higher. In the same way as our voice, the vibrations of thought carry the intention behind them. So if we are thinking negative thoughts about someone we are projecting negativity at that person. As a communication tool, we use telepathy more than we realise. It occurs more frequently within personal relationships or between parent and child. My partner will often say something I am thinking or we will have simultaneous ideas.

Visions are mental images of possible futures. The third eye is the design table where we sketch and refine our visions before building them in the outside world. With a vision, there is no attachment. It is a suggestion around which reality can be constructed. It is free to change, free to become more than the original idea. A vision works with Universal Creation, by giving it space to weave its magic. When we first have a vision we are simply required to bless it and blow it into the wind. Creation needs time to take that image and mix it together with other ingredients in ways that we could never have imagined possible. By developing patience and allowing our visions time to develop in the energetic world, we save our energy until the time arrives to act. The thing we have envisioned creating then already exists in the energetic realm, like a blue print. When we do act, the manifestation occurs almost without effort; it is supported from above. Oh, and remember to be careful what you ask for because you might just get it!

For a real insight into the manifestation of inner visions, read the personal autobiographies of Eileen and Peter Caddy about their vision that became the Findhorn Foundation in Scotland. It is an epic tale, a perfect example of allowing the universe to weave it's magic in unexpected ways coupled with the clarity and integrity of those involved. For those of you who have never heard of the Findhorn Foundation, it is a community in Scotland that was formed forty years ago. During the first fifteen years Eileen, Peter, their two children and friend Dorothy Maclean all lived in a small green caravan amongst sand dunes. Forty years later those same sand dunes are now thriving gardens and an international community, and it all came from a clear inner vision.

Before I wrote my first book I had the vision in my mind that I would write it; there was no doubt within me about it. I knew it would happen, I just didn't know how. I told the universe my only conditions were that I wanted a computer to write it on and I needed some support, as it was my first book. Then I just let it go and forgot about it. Six months later I received a cash windfall from a building society that had become a bank. This was a good sum of money and enabled me to buy a laptop computer and a printer. A few months later I was wondering around Ikea with a friend when my mobile phone rang. On the other end was the senior editor of a book packaging company in London. She said "You don't know me, but you have treated a friend of mine with Reiki. Would you be interested in writing a book for us?" She went on to say that they would provide the editor and design team and I would guide the process. I had the meeting, signed the contract and ten months later there was the book in my hands, an effortless display of manifestation.

What often prevents a vision manifesting itself is if the vision arises from the ego alone. The ego operates through need and want; it finds it difficult to let go of the control. The vision takes the form of a fantasy without a real willingness to surrender to the flow in order to achieve it. The Universe is not given the space to create because of the ego's control and attachment to how it wants it to be.

Synchronicity is an example of the images on our inner screen being matched by manifestation in the outer world. This will take the form of symbols and signs that when seen and acted upon take us on journeys we hadn't expected, but which are usually far richer than our intended journeys. When we open up to guidance our lives become infused with grace as if we are sitting in the palm of the Creator's hand. In order to be guided we need to be vigilant and open to seeing symbolic language.

In 1994 I was in Dingle Bay in southern Ireland. I was with four friends and we had journeyed there to swim with a wild dolphin called Funghi. At the end of our week we had run out of money, having only five pounds between us. We had return coach and ferry tickets from Kilmarnock so we weren't worried. When we arrived at the ferry terminal there were no more seats left on the coach and we couldn't board the ferry. We hadn't realised it was a public holiday and everyone, it appeared, was going to the UK. We asked if there was another ferry later that day and were told only from Dublin which was a six hour drive away, but there were no buses to Dublin. There were four of us and it was pouring with rain so hitch hiking wasn't an option. We decided to go to the café and bought tea and cakes with our last five pounds. None of us were concerned as the week had been such an adventure and this seemed in keeping with it. As we tucked into our tea and cakes we heard an announcement in a broad Irish accent over the public address system: "There is a

special bus service to Dublin leaving in five minutes from gate four."
We all looked at each other and shouted, "That's us!" Leaving our
unfinished feast, we ran to gate four and there to greet us was this
old 1940s bus with its driver smiling through thick glasses.

> *"You going to Dublin?" we asked.*
> *"That's me!" he replied. "Climb aboard!"*
> *"We haven't got any tickets," we said.*
> *"Oh you don't need tickets on my bus."*

So off we went to Dublin, just the four of us and the driver. He sang
Elvis songs to us the whole way on the microphone and even stopped
off to buy us all a Guinness. When we arrived that evening, there
were just four seats left on the coach that boarded the ferry to
London just for us. It turned out the driver had just dropped off
some people on a trip to Kilmarnock and it occurred to him that
there might be some people who needed a lift to Dublin.

In Reiki if we wish to send healing to somebody, we are required
to focus our mind on that person and lock on to him or her. Forgive
the analogy, but it's like a radar tracking system that locks on to a
target in order to fire a missile. Once we have that person locked
into our mind's eye, instead of firing a missile, we can send healing
from our heart and positive thoughts from our mind. The third eye
is the tool that we use to reach out into the subtle energy field to

connect to someone. The image of them will be displayed on our internal viewing screen. Through practise and discipline this tool can become highly effective.

In February 2001 I was teaching a Reiki class in Scotland and we decided to send healing to the victims of the earthquake that had struck the west coast of India about ten days earlier. As I connected to the event I suddenly had the image in my mind's eye of being trapped and in darkness. It was deeply disturbing and I had to will myself to stay focused on the image. I felt a lot of energy flowing through me for a good ten minutes and afterwards I shared what I had seen and experienced with the group. The next morning David who was in the group said, "Did you hear they pulled a woman out from the rubble alive last night?" I hadn't, but it was nice to hear and I allowed myself to think our little group had helped in some way. We can never know but it was a happy story.

IMBALANCES

As the function of the sixth chakra is to integrate the two functions of mind, imbalance occurs when the development of one aspect of mind occurs at the expense of the other. The two aspects are the male, logical, rational, linear mind and the female, intuitive, visual, abstract mind.

If the mind is too rational at the expense of the intuition, there will not be the willingness to see alternative points of view. The mind becomes blinkered and sceptical and adopts the 'I only believe what I can see with my own two eyes' syndrome. Suggest to such a person they actually have three eyes and they will look at you as if you're mad. There will be a lack of imagination. If you describe something to such a person, it will be difficult for them to visualise it within their own mind. They will lack the subtleties of communication. They won't get hints; they'll be the person who walks in on two people having a private conversation and won't realise. No consideration will be given to dreams or to intuitive impulses that arise from within. If there is a vision to create something it will be rushed without allowing the time to let it develop organically. They will deny alternatives, refusing to see other points of view. Such people built the Winchester by pass in England. They bulldozed their way through the most fragile and beautiful water meadows I have seen in England. They were not even prepared to entertain alternatives. The people who protested the building of the by pass were seen as environmental loonies. This is very sad but it appears that people who have lost touch with their intuitive mind run our present world. The straight lines and concrete structures of our modern world are a testament to a lack of imagination and creativity.

If the mind is so caught up in the fantasy and symbolic realms that it loses touch with rationality, we have another problem. Delusions are a result of a person living in a fantasy world that has no bearing on reality. They may have grand ideas for projects and things they wish to do, but never actually do any of them. They may be paranoid and believe in all kinds of conspiracies. Clairvoyance is a function of the feminine receptive mind. It is the ability to see psychic energy and read it. If there is a lack of balance in the sixth chakra there will be a tendency to lack discrimination. If there are unresolved emotional issue in the lower chakras for example, a person may get a sense of self-worth from giving psychic readings. What happens if no clear images come to mind? Will they make something up? Might they pluck something from the creative fantasy of their own mind to feel valid? This is a form of self-deception, the result of living in an illusory world. I was once invited for lunch by a born-again Christian. Just before we were about to eat, she said, "Did you hear that, there was a knock at the door?" I hadn't heard anything. She went to the door and opened it. When she came back she exclaimed with great delight, "Jesus has come for lunch!"

When we say 'The heart rules the head' we are referring to an emotive response to the decision-making process rather than a rational one. This shows how we have misunderstood both the nature of the heart and the mind. The heart is not our emotional centre; the second chakra has that attribute. Rationality makes up only half of the mind's function. If it were true of someone that their heart ruled their head, providing the heart was whole, we would find a person who would have clarity, love and truth as qualities of the mind.

If it is only the ego sitting in the driving seat then any personal observation will take place from a rational point of view. In order for true perception to take place we need to have a balance between the rational and the intuitive mind.

SELF-ASSESSMENT

Physical If you suffer frequent headaches, in particular migraines, there is a good chance there is an overload of psychic energy in the sixth chakra. This energy needs to be grounded down through the charkas. If there are unresolved issues further down, a person may have created a split in themselves and become top-heavy, living through the mind and denying themselves a physical existence. Inability to sleep and frequent nightmares are all related to an overactive sixth chakra. As vision is governed by this chakra, any sight related problems are related to the function of this centre.

Psychological/Emotional   People   with   emotional   and psychological issues related to the sixth chakra often create conflicts within their own minds when none actually exist. A sense of delusion surrounds this chakra if there is no balance. There is a tendency to perceive threats and develop incredible stories within the mind to give them credibility. People can become entrenched in mental patterns of despair that bring on psychological illnesses and depression. What we focus on with the mind, gives the object of our attention enormous power. If we use this chakra to focus on all that we perceive to be wrong with our lives, we give those issues more power and they continue to manifest. It is also through the mind that we disassociate ourselves from emotional traumas, or repress them allowing them to continue affecting us unconsciously.

EXERCISES

Distant Healing The Reiki art of sending healing requires a deep level of concentration on an event or person. The third eye is the instrument with which we focus our intent. Regularly practising this healing technique is great for the development of the sixth chakra.

Etheric gazing Take a partner and sit opposite each other. Relax and simply concentrate on looking at their third eye. Allow any shifts, images, visions or insights to come and go. Afterwards, share with each other what you saw.

7th Chakra: Sahasrara

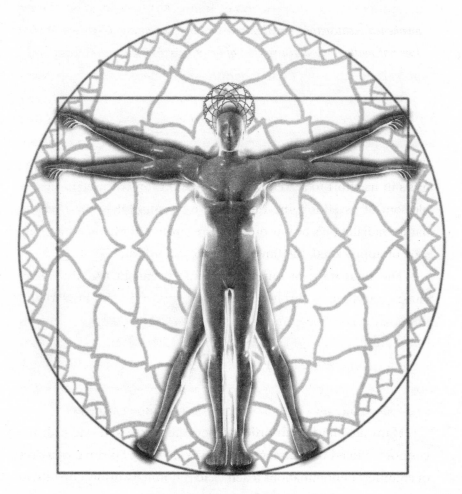

CROWN CHAKRA

"You can become massively awakened and still not be it. Seekers look for awakening but if there is no purity of heart you are worse off being awakened because then you'll think you have something when you don't. It does not matter how much you see of what is real if you are not being real."

John De Ruiter

When we look at a flower, it is comprised of a root system that connects deep into the earth and enables the flower to absorb the necessary nutrients for its survival. It has a stem, which turns and twists in its effort to search out the light. On top of the stem sits the blossom of its efforts, the flower. An expression of it's own inborn nature radiating it's beauty outwards, regardless of whether it is being seen or appreciated, the flower is complete and whole in itself.

The final stage of our journey that began in the Muladhara chakra and took us through the many twists and turns in search of our own light in the sixth chakra, is to now produce our own blossoming flower in the seventh chakra. This flowering expression takes the form of a fully integrated consciousness and as such one with the wholeness of the Cosmos. Such a flowering occurs within someone whilst they remain deeply rooted to the earth.

Many assume that in order to become whole and one with the cosmos we need to transcend the physical world. Spiritual practices of countless denominations teach us to renounce worldly pursuits, to transcend the body and to let go of our worldly possessions in order to gain enlightenment. This belief can create misunderstanding as it suggests the body and this world are all for nothing. I believe it is this notion that creates such disembodiment from our physical body and the earth and further separates us from each other. Imagine for a moment the opposite notion were true. What if the universe was created in order for consciousness to know itself? To dress itself in form, to be in a body, to taste, smell, feel, touch, love and cry. What if we need to be in all the pulls of this world in order to become conscious?

Would people, knowing themselves as an expression of God, be more mindful of how their actions impact on the world? If they recognised that same expression of God in others would they ever be able to kill in the name of God? I think not. The wars and conflicts of this earth fought in the name of the Almighty are a result of us externalising the god self, seeing the divine as something external, a higher power that we are beholden to. This is because we continue to have polarised views and we take these into the seventh chakra where the expression of duality doesn't exist.

A consequence of a polarised perception of creation is that religious doctrines often reflect that polarity. The most obvious of these is that God is an old man with a white beard sitting on a throne in paradise, judging us, and if he disapproves then off we go to the fiery furnace of eternal damnation. Now I might be in for quite a shock if that turns out to be true, but it doesn't appear to me to be a very holistic image of God. What it does represent is the ever-present duality of good versus evil, on which much of the western world is built. My experience of God is as a direct result of working with Reiki. What I know from that experience is God is Love not Justice. Whatever state I am in, when I open to Reiki, I am enveloped in absolute love, compassion and forgiveness. There are no conditions, simply a warm embrace and a welcome home.

The lack of wholeness in humanity is an indication that we are not yet home, we are not expressing our true nature, and we have not yet flowered. As consciousness we are still operating through beliefs and concepts that do not reflect reality and our perception of wholeness is from the outside looking in. That's like trying to know an ocean by sitting on a beach and looking at it. From the outside we can only imagine what it is like to surrender to the power of the ocean – far better to jump in and be a part of it, but that requires a leap of faith.

In order to be whole we must surrender ourselves to wholeness and this involves dissolving the boundaries that keep us separate. These boundaries exist in the ego. It is the ego's attachment to what and whom we have become that stops us surrendering. We have a personal investment in ourselves. It has taken us a lifetime to become us and our mind has refined and developed the package and is now attached to it. The very idea of letting go and surrendering to some infinite and indefinable power with no guarantees appals us. Once again, this is because we view that power as something outside us.

When we understand that we are sweetly surrendering to our own inner 'being-ness', allowing it to flower and fill the space that is us, then the leap into the ocean is simply us returning home, to what we know. We may still lose all that we have put together in our minds that we use to define ourselves, but it was never really worth anything anyway. What we lose is all the attachments that kept us separate from what we really are, an aspect of universal consciousness knowing itself.

So the purpose of the crown chakra is to liberate consciousness from the confinement of self-created identity by surrendering to our universal identity. In order for that to take place we need to let go of our attachments. But what does that mean? The danger in us attempting to let go of attachment to something is that we immediately replace it with something else. We can be attached to being someone and spend years striving to achieve it, then we suddenly decide in some great revelation to renounce all our worldly possessions, go to India and meditate all day on becoming no one. Now we have merely replaced our attachment to being 'somebody' with the attachment of being 'nobody'. Both require effort and once again reflect polarised views of reality.

Letting go of attachment requires no effort; it simply requires us to relax into existence as it is right now and let go of our control and desire for a set outcome. By being content with what is, we surrender to the wisdom of the universe and allow it to be our teacher.

A flower begins life as a seed, within which is contained it's potential. It becomes a flower because that is what it knows it should be. Our capacity as humans to be something we are not is what separates us from the rest of creation. We have the power to believe in what we want. We can make up an existence that fits in with the multitude of beliefs that we use to define ourselves. These beliefs generally come to us from outside. Each will require effort and control to maintain. They will require defending and justification. There is however a seed of unrealised potential within each one of us; the divine spark in each of us, our universal identity, which flowers through the understanding, gained in the crown chakra. Our potential, if realised, is to live in this world knowing that divine spark and letting that seed flower and be here on earth. It will then exist within us and be present in our body, our thoughts and our feelings.

IMBALANCES

The crown chakra is the final gateway through which we emerge as a flower of consciousness that has integrated the lessons contained within the previous chakras. We now have the possibility to know ourselves as an expression of the universe, liberated from self-identity.

Imbalances in the seventh chakra are created when the patterns of unconscious behaviour from the lower chakras are not integrated before this flowering takes place. If we move through this gateway as an unconscious, unbalanced and disintegrated being, what flowers will reflect just that. Whatever patterns of unconscious behaviour exist in our life, will continue to exist and repeat themselves over and over until such time as we can become conscious of them.

We may awaken to the idea that we have the potential to be a living, breathing expression of the universe but still not be it. If we remain attached to the very behaviour that prevents us actually being that expression it will remain only an idea. In order to become that expression we must allow consciousness to move into those patterns and in so doing liberate ourselves from them.

Without an open gateway to spirit, there will be a rejection of the subtle energies that make up this universe. The mind becomes entrenched within the boundaries of its material existence, refusing to accept the notion of a limitless expanse of consciousness in any form. If the mind does entertain such notions but remains attached to its self-created identity, it may become amazingly awakened to the nature of reality, but it will refuse to surrender itself. So as a consciousness it will not be integrating what it has realised.

When we become stuck in our beliefs we invariably feel the need to justify them. It is amazing to see how often we will rigorously defend a belief that serves only to limit us. If we approach someone to talk about a situation in our lives that limits us and a suggestion is made that may help us move out of the situation, we often move to justify its existence in our lives. We might say, "I know, I have tried that!" or " I can't do that!" or "It won't work!" or simply "I can't change." By doing this, we get stuck in the cycle of self-imposed limitation. This cycle always brings us back to where we started, which is complaining about what presently is.

The cycle goes as follows: dissatisfaction at what is, complaining or asking for help, being offered a solution, defending the limitation, justifying it's existence, affirming we do not intend to change, staying the way we are, complaining about what currently is, and around and around we go.

An attachment to a particular view is only seeing from a single perspective. It refuses to accept the possibility of alternatives. These attachments permeate through our everyday lives as we rigidly hold on to our beliefs and methods as if they are the only way to be, at the expense of an overall view. In order to let go of attachments it helps to have less personal investment in whatever it is we are believing, feeling, doing, owning or teaching, so that if it doesn't work out, is taken away or changes, we can be more open to what may replace it.

If it is true that we need to let go of attachments in order to allow a flowering of universal consciousness through us, it poses some interesting questions. Do meditators who have practised their discipline for years and years have to let go of their meditation practice in order to melt into the state of divine bliss? Do Buddhists who have arrived at the doorway to enlightenment by way of their practice have to let it go in order to step through the door? If that's the case, then whatever we are doing must remain playful otherwise it is difficult to let it go.

SELF-ASSESSMENT

Physical If you are out of touch with your body and live perpetually in your rational or intuitive mind, the liberating flow of universal energy cannot ground through your chakra system. Difficulties can surface anywhere along the central energy channel. Chronic migraines can be a consequence of energy not grounding and building up in the crown to produce severe pressure. This can result in confusion and disorientation. People with top-heavy energy often feel cold and cut off from the physical world. Crown chakra blockages also take the form of escapism. This can be in the form of drug abuse, spiritual extremism and denying the body its basic requirements in the search for purity.

Psychological/Emotional Crown chakra blockages can produce neurotic and compulsive behaviour. There will be a tendency to worry and the need to control all aspects of the environment. On the one hand there can be scepticism, rigid beliefs and a rejection of spiritual concepts; on the other a lack of discernment, delusion and escapism into the world of spirit at the expense of the physical and emotional.

EXERCISES

Surrendering To cultivate your connection to your higher self, decide to spend a day completely surrendering to your intuition. Whether it is deciding to go out or stay at home, go into a coffee shop, talk to someone or pick up a book, allow yourself to be guided and be vigilant to the signs and symbols that the universe shows you.

Meditation Meditate on the nature of impermanence. Close your eyes and breathe gently. Bring to mind all that is in your life – your possessions, family, friends, emotions, beliefs, ideals and your physical body. If all that were taken from you, what would be left?

The Head Stand A good physical exercise for the crown chakra is to do a headstand. If you find it difficult, try it against a wall or ask someone to support your legs for you.

The Complete System

We have discussed the chakras as individual centres of energy and hopefully gained an understanding of the various emotional, psychological and physical characteristics they contain. The chakra system, though made up of individual centres of spinning energy, operates as a whole and each centre, if out of balance, will affect the balance of the other chakras in the system. I have concentrated on the seven main chakras that run in a vertical line through the energy system, as the Reiki treatments also focus mainly on these. It is said there are 22 minor chakras which have similar roles to play as those of the main centres. I have already mentioned the chakras in the hands and feet, which are activated during the Reiki initiations. Other minor chakras of note are found either side of the solar plexus (Reiki position 9) in the *hara* or belly (Reiki position 10) and in the knees (Reiki position 13).

Energy is constantly flowing within this system both upwards and downwards, each chakra feeding into the one above and below it. The root chakra and the crown exchange energy with the earth and the universe as well as their neighbouring chakras. When the energy flow is uninhibited we experience ourselves free of stress, relaxed and with a sense of inner well-being. All these qualities amount to feeling harmonious within ourselves and as such we harmonise with our immediate environment, and from there the Earth and Universe. Any time there is a shift in the Universe you will be a part of it and experience it; any time there is a shift in the Earth the same is true. Any disharmony in any one chakra will be felt throughout the rest of your chakra system and affect the healthy functioning of the whole system.

You are made up of Earth, Water, Fire, Air, Space, Light and Consciousness.

These elements are combined in the greatest mystery of all – Your Life.

As you embrace Reiki you retune yourself with the universal tone of Love. You reclaim your place in the great orchestra of life. Your chakras are your own spiralling galaxies of light that connect you to all that is. Remember that each time you reach up to God, be as willing to dig your hands deep into the soil for you are as much a part of the Earth as you are the Light.

Energy Balancing Exercises
SPINNING SUFI EXERCISE

Stand with your right foot facing forwards and your left foot out to the left. Place your arms out horizontally and look ahead fixing your eyes on a point. Spin clockwise to your right as fast as is comfortable and keep your focus on the point you have chosen until it is no longer possible then allow your head to turn a full revolution, bringing your

SPINNING

eyes back to the same point of focus as before, like a dancer on ice. At first, spin a maximum of 7 times then crouch on the floor head down and breathe slowly. Once you have got used to the exercise you can increase the number of spins to a maximum of 21 times.

It is believed this exercise helps the chakras to rotate and balance. Advanced use of this exercise, when the person spins hundreds of times, is said to produce a trance-like state. It is interesting to observe that children spin as a form of play without any side effects. As adults we may find this exercise produces nausea, but with perseverance it can be a useful chakra-balancing exercise.

BREATHING PURIFICATION EXERCISE

Sit in a comfortable position keeping the back straight. Relax the hands and place them on your lap. Breathe in, visualising a stream of rainbow colours flowing through you from the crown. Beginning with the base chakra, exhale with your mouth open in four bursts to correspond with the four petals of the chakra. Breathe in again and concentrating on the second chakra exhale in six bursts. Inhale again and focus on the third chakra. Breathe out in ten bursts. Inhale and focus on the fourth chakra. Exhale in twelve bursts. Breathe in again and focus on the fifth chakra. Exhale in sixteen bursts. Breathe in and now focus on the sixth and seventh chakras together. Exhale in two bursts.

Repeat the whole exercise three times. It is important to exhale constantly without taking another breath for each chakra. You will have to try to gauge the amount of air you exhale in each burst so you don't run out of air.

This exercise is said to balance physical and mental energy, strengthen the nervous system, help memory and concentration and eliminate toxins and impurities.

The only side effect is that you can over-oxygenate, in which case lie down and try the exercise again the following day.

KI EXERCISE

How much Ki can you generate? Stand with your feet shoulder-width apart, knees bent, arms by your side. Relax your stomach and breathe in through your nose. Exhale through your mouth. As you breathe in and out feel the energy building in your hands – normally heat or tingling. Try to concentrate and draw energy in. Slowly allow your hands to rise up from your sides and hold them out in front of you. Keep breathing and relaxing. Visualise yourself suspended in water and supported by it. If you are generating enough Ki the feeling of floating will be so strong you will be able to keep your arms up all day, if not you will get tired pretty quickly

HOW MUCH KI ARE YOU LEAKING?

Try to visualise yourself from afar. See yourself standing feet apart with Ki in the form of light entering into you from above and filling your energy system. As you visualise this, observe to see if light leaks from your system. Does it? Where and how much? Does it pour out of you? Does it flow to a memory, another time, a place, and a person? There are thousands of ways that we leak energy. Any time we let ourselves be scattered and try to focus on too many things at once, they require energy.

LEAKING LIGHT

The Full Treatment And The Seven Chakras

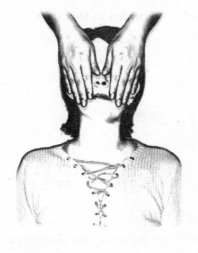

POSITION 1

Over the forehead, eyes and cheeks

Works on eye problems, sinuses, colds, allergies, nerves in the brain, pituitary and pineal gland. Balances the pineal gland, which is the centre of hormonal regulation. This position helps relax the client and stimulates and balances sixth chakra.

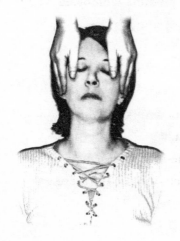

POSITION 2

To the sides of the temples

Works on the optic nerves and balances the right (Intuition, Wisdom) and left (Rational understanding) sides of the brain. This position is very relaxing in cases of stress.

POSITION 3

Over the ears

Treats many organs via the
acupuncture points in this area.
These include the heart, intestines,
kidneys, lungs, stomach, liver and
gall bladder.

This position helps to balance.

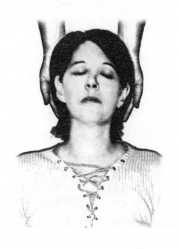

POSITION 4

**The back of the head, the fingertips
on the Medulla Oblongata**

Works on the eyes, vision,
headaches, nosebleeds, stroke and
pineal gland.

It is the memory bank for all
childhood and past life emotional
trauma.

The Medulla Oblongata is
connected to the third eye.

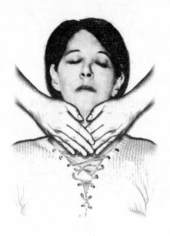

POSITION 5
The Throat, 5th Chakra
Treats sore throat, flu, high blood pressure, anger, frustration, problems with expression of one's truth and the thyroid gland, which affects metabolism.

The Throat Chakra affects communication and creativity.

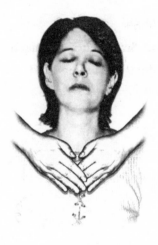

POSITION 6
The Thymus Gland/Upper Chest.
This is where we feel fear, panic, stress and emotions and is known as the survival spot. Affects energy levels.

People often feel a sense of suffocation in this area when their Heart Chakra closes. Reveals problems in relating to others.

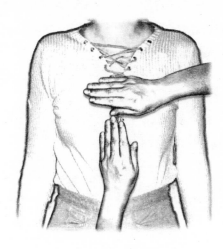

POSITION 7

Heart 4th Chakra/T-Position

Treats emotional blockages, circulation, and stress and heart problems.

This chakra affects our ability to love ourselves and others on all levels.

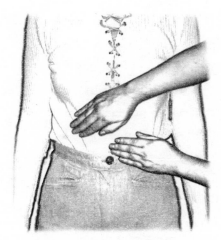

POSITION 8

Solar Plexus 3rd Chakra/Stomach

Works on the digestion and old patterns, where we receive from the outside.

This is our feeling and worry centre.

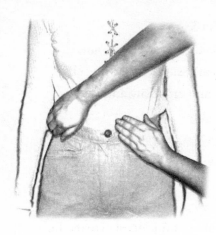

POSITION 9

Liver and Spleen

Treats suppression of anger, bitterness, sadness and depression and codification on all levels. Includes the gall bladder and pancreas.

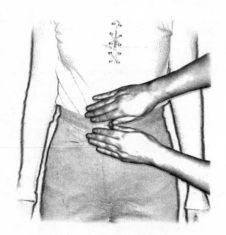

POSITION 10

Hara/ Belly

This deals with suppression of all issues relating to power and treats the intestines and duodenum.

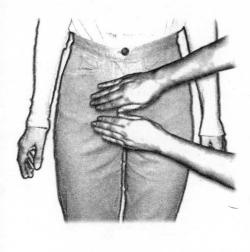

POSITION 11
2nd Chakra

Treats all issues to do with self-worth and creativity and on physical, mental, emotional and spiritual problems due to misalignment with Mother Earth. Assists in the extreme storage of suppressed sexual issues such as rape, abuse and incest. Treats the sexual organs, prostrate, bladder, ovaries, urethra and appendix.

Chakra Harmonising

Place your hands above the body at the 1st and 6th chakras, then move your hands together and place them over the 2nd and 5th chakras, then finally over the 3rd and 4th chakras. Hold your hands in each position for approximately 1–2 minutes or until you feel ready to move on.

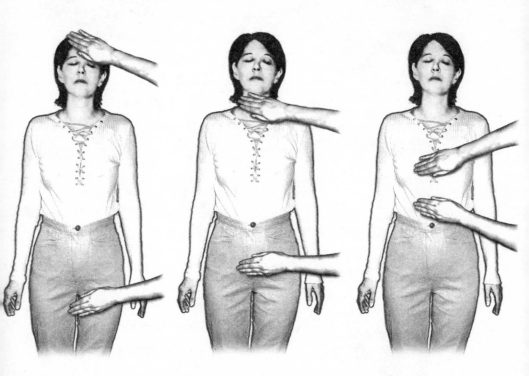

POSITION 12
Shoulders & Arms
This connects the main Heart and Colon Meridians and helps to comfort client.

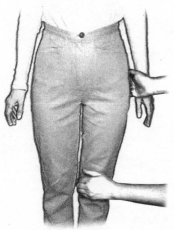

POSITION 13
Hips & Knees
Helps with sciatica, arthritis and joint pains in general.

This is another emotional storage area. Stiffness in this area can suggest problems with changing beliefs and moving forward.

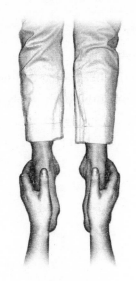

POSITION 14

Feet

The feet contain meridian points, which relate to all parts of the body. Holding the feet helps to ground the client.

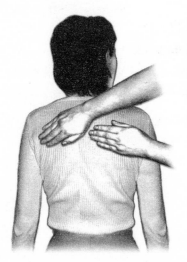

Back

POSITION 1

Shoulders

Helps to relieve stress built up in this area.

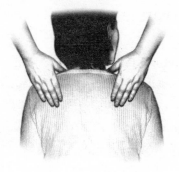

POSITION 2
Upper Back/Lung

Relates to the heart, so all ailments on the front of the body apply. It is very helpful to patients suffering from bronchial problems.

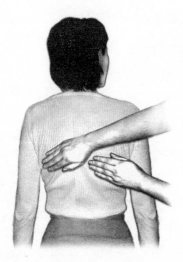

POSITION 3
Middle Back/Lung

Relates to the solar plexus, so all ailments on the front of the body apply.

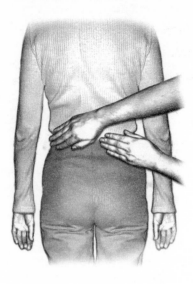

POSITION 4

Lower Back

Relates to 2nd chakra, so all ailments on the front of the body apply.

It is also helpful for sciatica.

This is a main emotional storage area.

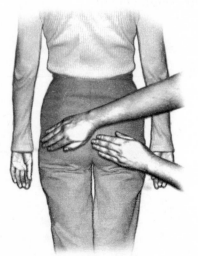

POSITION 5

Buttocks.

As above.

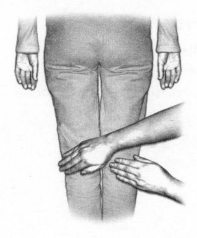

POSITION 6

Backs of knees

(secondary chakras)

POSITION 7.

Feet

Helps to ground client

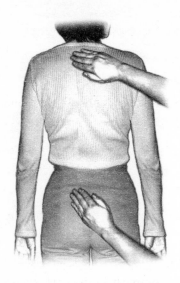

POSITION 8

Coccyx & Top of Spine/7th Vertebrae

Helps to run energy through the spine to move any blocks that may exist there.

Reiki Dos & Don'ts

There are no known contraindications for Reiki, and the following are simply precautions that are advised by Reiki masters.

When treating a broken bone or fracture always ensure the bone is set in a cast first. This is because the efficiency of Reiki to heal the bone is remarkable in the early stages, and if the bone is not set properly it may heal incorrectly and need to be re-broken and re-set.

Caution should be taken when treating people who are fitted with artificial devices such as pacemakers as Reiki could affect the device.

Be careful when treating pregnant women. Most alternative therapies are cautious in this situation, particularly in the early stages of pregnancy, in case of miscarriage after a treatment. I have heard of no such case with Reiki though I advise you to proceed with care.

When treating people with diabetes, advise patients that Reiki has been shown to affect the levels of insulin required by the body.

- Avoid giving Reiki after drinking alcohol.
- Avoid giving Reiki to someone else who is under the influence of alcohol or drugs.

Remember when giving Reiki, to release yourself from any sense of responsibility regarding the outcome of the healing. As channels of Reiki, we are simply observers of what is taking place and can therefore allow ourselves to be guided. The more empty we can become by letting go of our own need of a positive outcome, the more effective we are. It is worth observing oneself whilst giving a treatment to see if there is any personal investment regarding the outcome of the healing. If you find any residue of this don't be hard on yourself as it is a human characteristic to want to help people, but try to let it go and simply trust that if the time is right Reiki will provide the impulse to heal.

The Seventh Chakra And The Initiation

The only time we use the crown chakra in Reiki is when giving the Reiki initiations of all levels. I know of some people who treat this chakra in cases of chronic migraine, but there are no set positions for the crown chakra. The general thinking behind this is that the crown centre, being the connection to the Universal Spirit, should not really be interfered with. During an initiation, both the student and initiating master are really surrendering to the flow of energy that comes from the Reiki lineage and their higher selves. The effect of this energy entering the crown centre always amazes me. Being involved as a channel for this energy, there is a very real feeling of the presence of the masters' lineage. It is very different from a healing, and my experience is that if I carry any issues into an initiation they are quickly exposed and released. I feel that one of the greatest gifts I have been given in this life is the ability to pass on Reiki initiations. Whenever I give an initiation, I can feel myself being re-tuned and realigned along with the student.

With regard to treating migraine through the crown centre, I have found through experience that for any real long-lasting relief, the lower chakras need to be treated. Migraine appears to be the result of too much crown chakra activity, with nowhere for the excess energy to go because the lower chakras are blocked. Once they are clear, the energy from the crown is able to circulate again which relieves the pressure in the head.

Second Degree Reiki

As we move into second level Reiki we are introduced to the symbols discovered by Dr Usui in his vision. I describe these symbols as the three golden keys of Reiki. Each key has a specific purpose and though they carry an inherent vibration in themselves, it is the initiation given in second degree Reiki that empowers their use.

They are as follows:

THE POWER SYMBOL
This is the key that brings power to our intention.
Through it's shape and mantra, it connects us to the universal pattern of creation – the spiral. This symbol is used to increase energy flow and acts as a seal for the other second-degree symbols. It is used to cleanse and protect objects and spaces.

THE EMOTIONAL/MENTAL SYMBOL
This is the key to our unconscious.
A symbol that reminds us that it is our emotional and mental patterns that keep us separate from our true nature. The formation of the emotional body is linked to the first three chakras, the formation of the mental body to the top three chakras. The heart

links the emotional and mental bodies together. This symbol helps us to unite the emotional and mental planes.

THE DISTANT HEALING SYMBOL
This represents the key to time and space.
This symbol reminds us that time and space are an illusion. Through it we can access a person or event and send healing beyond time and space.

In addition to the symbols, we are given the techniques to send healing to a person or event anywhere in time and space. We are shown another healing treatment to access the unconscious patterns in the emotional and mental body. We are shown how to use the power symbol for protection and to clear and prepare healing spaces.

Symbology
Symbols are the language of the soul and spirit. Even the earth uses symbols to communicate to us. We have been used to the Earth communicating to us through unsophisticated symbolic language such as earthquakes and volcanoes. Increasingly though, the earth is presenting us with more sophisticated forms of communication. Symbols appear each year in the wheat fields of southwest England in the form of crop circles. These intricate symbols seem to speak to

our soul and appear familiar as if we have seen them before. Though we may not understand them with our rational mind, nevertheless they touch us. They speak of other dimensions of reality that we forget in the humdrum of everyday life. Marko Pokajnick teaches that crop circles are the earth's way of communicating with our own earth-bound nature, our physical and elemental selves. They open up something within us; they talk to a part of us deep inside and long forgotten. They remind us that life is a mystery to be discovered rather than a business to be managed.

In the Reiki community we have four symbols that are given to us. Three of them are given in second level and the fourth symbol is given to masters of Reiki. Ultimately, all the Reiki symbols are our way of affirming our Universal identity. I deliberated about drawing them here for you all, but decided I didn't want to betray the trust of my master. I told her I would keep them a secret and so I will. They are hardly a secret these days, and if you don't know them it's pretty easy to find them in various forms on the Internet and in other books published on Reiki. What has come to light in recent years is that there are many different ways in which symbols are drawn. Some masters declare theirs to be more powerful than others and so on. This all leads to a climate of confusion within the Reiki community. I personally think it's all talk and not worth worrying about. These symbols are drawn for us in the way they have been drawn for our masters all the way back to Dr Usui. Just as no two people write the same way, no people draw the same way; so the symbols as drawn by western people have changed over time, but this does not change their intention.

The inclusion of these symbols in our healing art occurred as a result of the vision Dr Usui had. There are conflicting stories as to how they appeared to him. Some say they were written in gold in the sky after Dr Usui was rendered unconscious by a blinding light, others that he received the vision during a fever. However they appeared to him, they have become a defining part of the Reiki practice. As we have learned, symbols are the language of the upper three chakras, whether they take the form of sounds, pictures or intuitive flashes of light and colour. Through the spoken or written word we can bring the clarity of mind to paper. By intentionally focusing our mind directly towards a person or event, we can communicate energetically and transmit our intention in thoughts and feelings. The symbols are given to aid this process.

Distant Healing

"There is no past and there is no present and there is no future, for even time itself is an illusion and by a single clap of the hand, it too can be returned to the void." Dr Usui

When we begin to understand existence as form manifested within a vibratory field of consciousness, it is only a small step to realising that our thoughts and feelings can have an influence on that field. As we have learned, our intention carries a charge that accompanies whatever it is we are presently doing. This charge can impact on the physical through our actions, or more subtly on the energy around us. Whenever we think of others we are communicating with them. Depending on the nature of our thoughts and the emotional charge that accompanies them, the person on whom we are focused will receive either positive or negative vibrations. The amount of psychic energy we put into focusing on them will determine whether they are aware of it or not. Unfortunately, most of us only experience this when we are in conflict with someone. Think back to the last time you had an argument with someone. How much energy did you project towards him or her? What were the nature of the thoughts and feelings you sent? How did it make you feel? If we are to embrace the concept of distant healing, the sending of love and light to a person, we first have to become aware of our negative projections at other times.

When we are stuck in a conflict, generally what we really want to do is communicate clearly our hurt or frustration, be heard and try to gain some understanding. What gets in the way is the pride and stubbornness of our ego. In other words, we go back into our self-created identities. The ego with all its polarised views of reality finds it difficult to admit there might be another perspective. For this reason, distant healing is a really useful tool to have, especially in disharmonious situations. If when conflict with someone arises you focus on them and send love, light and healing rather than negative projections, the chance of conflict resolution increases dramatically. Whilst connected to Reiki we are surrounded by an energy that is just so forgiving that it becomes impossible to maintain negative feelings about someone. In workshops I ask people to name someone they would like to send love and light to at the end of each session. Each person say's a name and then we blow the light of the candle that has been burning throughout the session to them. The person that light is sent to is invariably in conflict with a member of the healing circle that named them. This shows that at the root of all conflict there is a willingness to forgive and form new bridges out of love and light.

So when we choose to send healing to someone, it is the focus we bring to that act that determines the success of it. The chakras directly involved in this process are the third eye, the heart and the throat. The third eye brings focus to our intention by visualising the person or event we wish to send the healing to. It is good to remember at this stage that the element of the third eye is light. Confucius once wrote: "It is better to light a single candle than curse the darkness." In the shining of light into darkness we bring about illumination, we can see clearly what is really there. So by focusing the light of our third eye on a person or event we can help to bring clarity and understanding to a situation. The throat's element is ether, so through this centre we connect etherically to the person or event. The throat chakra can also be used to vocalise our intention, by naming the person with whom we wish to connect. Once we have formed the connection with our third- eye and throat centres and are able to maintain it with concentration, we can let the loving emanations that flow through the heart from creation breathe new life into the situation.

In Reiki the distant healing symbol is our way of creating true intention, by ensuring the flow of energy comes from our universal selves. The symbol forms a bridge between our self-created identity and our universal identity or higher self. The distant healing symbol reminds us that the only moment in creation is now! All of creation is accessible through being in the now! Time and space define our physical limitations and restrict our physical bodies, but our spirit is only limited by our beliefs.

For the distant healing technique, draw the symbols in the following sequence:

- The name of a person or event 3 times
- The Power symbol 3 times
- The Emotional/Mental symbol 3 times
- The Power symbol 3 times
- The Distant symbol 3 times
- The Power symbol 3 times.

Clearing Spaces With Reiki

I believe it's important to develop our sensitivity and awareness in environments that do not invade and clutter our energy fields, but instead help us feel safe and open enough to nurture this capability. If you want to listen to the sound of a butterfly's wings flapping you don't stand next to a man beating a drum! Once developed and anchored in us, we can then further develop our sensitivity by maintaining that level of openness in less supportive environments.

It's always nice to return to a safe place, whether it is a healing room, your front living room or a bedroom. These spaces feel safe to us because they reflect our personal vibration. They hold a residue of our energy signature; to return to them is to feel our own energy again, rather than the numerous energies we come into contact with during our day.

We can use the power symbol to help clear spaces of disharmonious energies that might exist there. This can be a place you intend to use for healing and meditation, or simply to maintain a clear energy in your office or home. In much the same way as we use the three chakras of heart, throat and third eye for distant healing, the same applies in energy clearing exercises. If you sit or stand centrally in the room and allow yourself to tune in to what is there, you may find you experience the disharmonious energies within your own field. That's okay. Once you are aware of what exists, you can then do something to change it. Begin by calling on your guides, helpers and the Reiki energy. Focus your attention on purifying the energy that is present. Visualise a stream of light containing all the colours of the rainbow flowing through your chakra system. Allow your heart to expand with these energies and from here flow out into the room. Try to visualise the whole room filling up with these colours. Once you feel the room flood with these new energies, visualise the power symbol and mentally draw it into the four corners of the room, sealing the new energies in. Alternatively, you can actually stand up and physically draw the power symbol into each corner of the room.

For sealing a healing space or protecting an object:
- Seal your intent with the Power symbol 3 times.

Psychological/Emotional Healing

"I suddenly realised to my amazement I was not thinking – I was being thought." Byron Katie

The psychological/emotional healing technique uses the emotional/mental symbol drawn directly into the third eye. The intention is to help facilitate the release of emotional energies repressed by the mind. If there is a release it will take the form of a memory of an event being recalled from the unconscious mind. Emotional releases usually follow.

During a second-level workshop I had introduced this healing technique and asked the students to practise. Within a few moments of starting, a young woman started to cry. I went over to see if I could help in some way and intuitively started beaming Reiki into the second chakra region. She opened her eyes and shouted, "Get away, get away!" I could tell she wasn't seeing me anymore but someone else. I reassured her by saying that it was me, Richard, and that seemed to bring her back to the present again. She went on to release deep emotions. Afterwards she shared that she had seen herself being abused as a young girl, and when she opened her eyes I appeared to her as the man who had carried out the abuse.

I must admit I found the process deeply unsettling. Maybe in some way I had experienced the strain of distorted energy that is prevalent in men who carry out such abuse.

This healing technique is very powerful and even if deeply buried memories do not surface, quite often a person is taken on a symbolic dream-like journey in the mind by the Reiki energy.

For the mental/emotional healing technique, draw the symbols in the following sequence and place the hands to the back and front of the third eye:

- The name of the person 3 times
- The Power symbol 3 times
- The Mental/Emotional symbol 3 times
- The Power symbol 3 times

Diagnostic Dowsing

Dowsing is a traditional method of diagnosis or divination as old as time. It is used to find energy lines in the earth, power points and even water. A dowsing instrument – usually a crystal on the end ofthread – can be used to determine the balance of the individual chakras by simply suspending it in each chakra's energy. It is important to determine a yes/no response from the crystal first, by simply asking it for the movement response for positive or negative. Once established, the crystal can be held above a chakra and asked

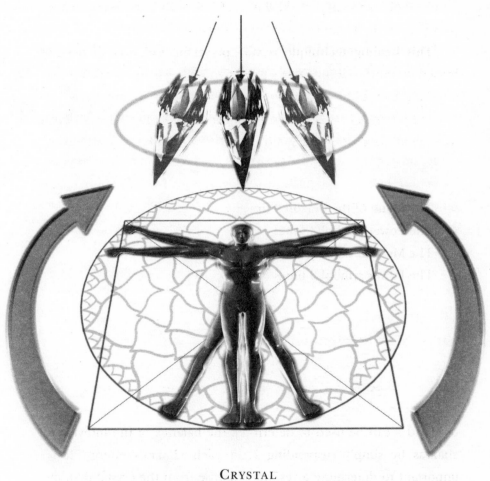

CRYSTAL

if the chakra is balanced. If the crystal indicates "No", you can ask if the energy of the chakra is excessive or insufficient.

After working with the dowsing crystal for a time, observe yourself to see if the crystal response is the same as your intuitive response. Focus your attention on the same part of your own body as you hold the dowsing crystal in the other person's chakra. If the energy in your own body shifts, it is an indication that you are empathising with the other person. In time, you will be able to dowse someone's chakra system with your own body by feeling the effects they have on your energy field.

Reiki in Life

The Collective Energy Field

*"Everyone is a river flowing from the past to the future. The water that
flows in one river is of the same substance as the water that flows
in all rivers." Dr Usui*

My understanding of the human energy field is that it is a
subtle extension of our physical self that reaches out and
communicates on an intuitive level with other such subtle fields of
energy around it. Everything alive, including the Earth itself, has this
subtle field of energy surrounding it. To be on this earth is to swim
within the currents of a vast ocean of energy made up of thoughts
and emotions. Our individual contribution to that collective field of
energy is our responsibility alone. Therefore it is absolutely vital that
we have some comprehension of what is taking place. The easiest
way to observe the potential influence of a collective field on an
individual is in world crises. On September 11, 2001, we all watched
in horror as terror reigned down from the skies in the form of
hijacked airliners aimed deliberately at the twin towers of the World
Trade Centre in Manhattan, New York and the Pentagon in
Washington D.C. As the reality of what had taken place sunk in, the

emotional shock wave that was felt around the globe was enormous. The image that came to mind for me was of a black hole sucking life force into it. I could see how that black hole created by the actions of the terrorists was now being maintained and fed by the emotions experienced by us, the millions of global viewers. Rather than going into the shock and drama of what had taken place, it was important to feed the situation with Love and Light, to facilitate healing in much the same way we would someone coming to us on an individual basis for the healing of shock or emotional trauma. I am sure this took place on a small scale. However, for those who got pulled into the drama, the consequences were emotional exhaustion as their personal energy fields were pulled on and flooded with the full horror of what had taken place. As human consciousness evolves towards peace there are going to be huge numbers of people that resist that evolution. The resisting will take on the form of terrorism and acts such as we saw on that day in September. What is vital for us is how we respond to such dramas that threaten our safety and security. It is easy to give healing when we are on a beautiful retreat and all is well with the world. However, in times of world crises it is even more important that we respond by focusing our hearts and minds towards healing and not panic.

Protection

"Suppose you could find a simple way to embrace your life with joy, stop arguing with reality, and achieve serenity in the midst of chaos? That is what Loving What Is offers." Erica Jong

I wish to talk about protection in terms of creating a harmonic resonance between any potential conflict we may face and ourselves. Usually when we think of protection we think in terms of erecting imaginary barriers between the source of discomfort and ourselves. This suggests our state of openness or oneness is dependent on the situation we find ourselves in. We demonstrate how conditional our openness is by way of preference, but in doing so we constantly affirm our separateness. We want to be open and harmonious but when we meet people who are closed and disharmonious we move to protect ourselves in order to maintain our sense of harmony. We become victims of circumstance and our position becomes one of defence.

Normally, when in conflict with someone we feel it in our solar plexus. The third chakra responds by contracting. If the conflict is long-lasting, this contraction will result in physical symptoms in any of the organs governed by this chakra. Energy flow will also be inhibited to the other chakras in the system. So it is important to find a way of remaining open in situations that would ordinarily cause us to close down.

One useful truth I apply is that if I see this in someone else, it resides in me. I can't change them, but I can change myself.

In Reiki we are given a great tool that can be brought to situations of conflict. This tool is the Power symbol. I started this book with the story of its effectiveness on the aircraft in Hawaii. We have learned it can be used to protect objects and help to seal a sacred space. It can also be used to help diffuse conflicts. It does this not by erecting obstacles, but by introducing harmony to the situation. When visualised and directed towards a person it doesn't create separation but simply brings power to the situation. I have found that by directing this symbol towards another person's solar plexus chakra, it appears to remove the emotional charge that creates contraction in me. As what I am sending to the person is a symbol of universal harmony, there is no malice in the intention. Rather there is the conscious intent to place between us a space for understanding. The effectiveness of this technique is dependent on your ability to visualise and project clearly whilst in the midst of conflict. If it is unsuccessful then you simply find yourself in the same position as you were before and you can try again.

Reiki With Nature

"As soon as you are not at one with what is real, you will be profoundly not okay." John de Ruiter

Reiki teaches us that all pain, all suffering and illness are born out of separation. But how can we be separate from creation when we live in it? It is hard to believe that whilst living on this planet we can be separate from it, but how often are you aware of the cycles of the moon? Do you feel the sadness of a dammed river or the desolation of a decimated forest? When you are stuck in a tailback and you can't go anywhere, do you wonder if humanity has gone mad? When you gaze into the night and cannot see the stars for the lights of our cities, how does it make you feel? Have you ever stopped and been overwhelmed by the majesty of an oak tree, seen the sun setting into the ocean, smelt the rain? Have you ever really stopped for a while and listened to what your heart is telling you? The illusion of reality that we create for ourselves is a major cause of our separation; it contributes to our suffering and yet we continue to create it, all the while knowing in our heart it is not real. By re-establishing our connection to the Earth we re-connect to our earth nature. Our whole energetic system connects into the earth and just as we respond to the healing energy of Reiki, so too does the Earth.

There are many ways that Reiki can be used to give healing to nature. We can begin by simply giving energy to our houseplants as we water them. We can become more conscious of nature in our environment as we walk around and simply send love to it. We can go to power points on the Earth and consciously bring Reiki into those areas by being channels for energy to flow into the Earth as it is needed, in the same way we would the chakras of the body. We can apply distant healing techniques to crises around the world such as earthquakes, wars, famine, floods or injustices. Whenever such crises occur on this planet we always have the choice of being a part of the drama, the politics and the arguments, or being a channel for sending love; it is far better to choose the latter.

Honouring Reiki

"The genius of consciousness has the power to make something up, believe in it and live it as though it were really true. What is so wonderful is that it never works." John De Ruiter

In any discipline or form of healing we never stand still; we are constantly growing and evolving in our understanding of what the discipline involves. Sometimes this creates a conflict between the original teachings and the expansion of understanding we gain through the application of those teachings. In the seven years that I have been involved with Reiki, one recurring theme I have seen, has been the diversity of ways in which it is taught and applied. I find when teaching second degree and master degree students who have taken the previous levels with another teacher, that they have different approaches to Reiki. They have been given strict guidelines of what and what not to do. Some have received Reiki One and Two in a weekend; others in a single day. Some have received an initiation and nothing else; others a very thorough training.

This lack of legislation in the way Reiki is taught has been the source of many discussions within the Reiki community. Phyllis Furumoto, the widely recognised grand master of the western tradition of Reiki, has tried recently to trademark the name Reiki in an effort to police this healing art. I am happy to say this endeavour has not been successful. What is apparent to me is that Reiki's present disarray points in part towards discomfort with the present structure, in particular the issue of the financial implications of becoming a Reiki master.

The essence of Reiki is formless. Since its discovery by the West, the Reiki that is being presented to the world has been formalised so the western mind can comprehend it. Its essence is often forgotten in the raging arguments about who is in charge, which is the right technique, which lineage you belong to and so on. It is time to live what we teach and apply our philosophy to the present conflicts within the Reiki community, by releasing issues of power, control, fear and structure and gently allowing Reiki to heal itself. We must simply stop trying to hold it in a pattern that it does not belong in. The essence of Reiki is Truth. Let us drink its essence.

When giving a treatment, this struggle between form and freedom is easily seen. You can find yourself following a set of hand positions and yet your intuition is screaming at you to go straight to the relevant point that needs attention. Personally I have found that when I am truly empty and allow myself to dance with the energy, then the rigid confines of a set of hand positions serve very little purpose. All that happens is that they bring me back into a mental state of 'should be doing' rather than the 'being' state of healing. If we are healing, it is a momentary experience we find ourselves in with the person who is being healed. We do not remain healers once that moment is passed. If we try to do so we are merely allowing ourselves to become attached to the idea that we are healers.

To give healing is to hold a space of intention in which healing may occur. The person who receives healing within that space is he who is open to receive. It is just as possible that the healer is the one to be healed as it is the receiver. When we give healing it is worth remembering that intimate oneness exists not only between the Universe and ourselves, but also between us and the person lying down to receive. Invariably, as the holders of a healing space, we have as much to learn and receive as those that lay down in trust on our tables. If we view our healing sessions with Reiki in this way, it is possible that the level of energy and healing we receive will offset the need for some financial compensation to honour our work.

It is important to honour ourselves, our work, our space and our teachings, and I believe that people have the capacity to know what is correct within themselves; they don't need a doctrine to tell them. Reiki is not a business; it is a healing art. Dr Usui's fourth principle was: *'Earn your living honestly'*. People will respect Reiki not because we place a value on its head, but because it is taught with love and honesty.

A Prayer

Dr Mikao Usui gave us a prayer, which he took directly from the sacred Buddhist texts. It is as follows:

"We bow down, offer incense and pray to the Medicine King Buddha, Lord of Healing, Lord of the Lapis Lazuli Light.

Throughout the ten directions and Three Times, may sickness be a name, a word heard no more. May suffering be only a dark memory; may diseases be banished from the hearts and minds of all sentient beings.

May all people gain health, well-being, peace and prosperity. Thus, may the great Blessing Storehouse of the Buddhas pour forth a rain of auspiciousness to those who hear and read these words."

Extract from Medicine Dharma Reiki by Lama Yeshe

A Modern History

This following account was written and compiled by Lawrence Ellyard, author of "The Tao of Reiki" Full Circle Publishing. The content of this information extends to a variety of sources. Further information can be found at www.taoofreiki.com

The Life Story of Dr Usui

Mikao Usui was born in the village of Yago in the Gifu Prefecture on August 15, 1865, where his ancestors had lived for eleven generations. His family belonged to the Tendai sect of Buddhism. When he was four, he was sent to a Tendai Monastery to receive his primary education.

Usui pursued higher education and received a doctorate in literature. He spoke many languages and became well-versed in medicine, theology and philosophy. Like many intellectuals of his day, Usui was fascinated with the 'new science' coming from the West. During this time (1880s and 90s), the Meiji Emperor had begun a new regime that overthrew the Shoguns and Japan's feudal states, now relocated in Tokyo, and were brought under the direct control of the central government. Under this new regime, the 'old ideas' were discarded in favor of modernisation and the country was opened to westerners for the first time. There rose frenzy for transforming the modes of daily life into occidental fashions, which were identified with civilisation. In every department of social and political life, men furnished with some knowledge of modern science were promoted to high positions. Men of 'new knowledge' were almost idolised and the ambition of every young man was to read the 'horizontal writings' of occidental books. The nation as a whole asked eagerly for the benefits of the new civilisation. The motto of the era was 'Enlightenment and Civilisation'.

Usui's father, Uzaemon, was an avid follower of the new regime and adopted progressive political views. Usui had great respect for his father and was very influenced by this national obsession to become 'westernised'. Usui continued to study science and medicine. In addition, he befriended several Christian missionaries who had studied medicine at Harvard and Yale. Usui learnt much from these western missionaries and their knowledge and tuition became the basis for much of his learning.

During this time when Japan was opening its doors to the West, the first arrivals were the missionaries, both Catholic and Protestant. They set up their operations in three main areas. One was in Yokohama, under the influence of Rev. John Ballagh. Here they started their medical work and brought with them knowledge of western medical science. These missionaries became very influential leaders and formed the first Japanese Christian church in 1872.

Throughout Usui's early adulthood, he lived in Kyoto with his wife, Sadako Sizuki, and two children, a son and a daughter. He continued his religious study and became involved with a group named 'Rei Jyutsu Ka'. This group had a centre at the base of the holy mountain, Kurama Yama, north of Kyoto. There is an ancient Buddhist temple, Kurama-dera on the 1,700 ft mountain which has a large statue of Amida Buddha and houses many artifacts that are part of the National Treasure. Built in 770AD, the temple belonged to the Tendai sect of esoteric Buddhism. By 1945 the temple had evolved into an independent Buddhist sect. For centuries, Kurama has been regarded as a spiritual place and many famous sages, as well as Emperors, go there to pray. The temple and surrounding areas are kept in their natural state and the mountain itself is the spiritual symbol of Kurama temple. Steps lead down to the base where one can sit and meditate. Nearby is a waterfall. Usui reportedly went to this area frequently to meditate.

It was during this time (c.1888) that Usui contracted Cholera as an epidemic swept through Kyoto. He had a profound near death experience in which he received a vision regarding his life's purpose. During his revelations, it became known to him that it was his purpose to create a system of healing to benefit humanity, the Buddha of healing appeared to him and told him that it was his life purpose to create a system of healing that utilised modern and ancient teachings. The following morning, much to the surprise of his attendants and family, Usui quickly recovered from his illness. This was a life changing experience for Usui that caused him to make a major reassessment of his life-path and direction. He soon developed a keen interest in the esoteric science of healing as taught by the Buddha, and he developed the compassionate wish to learn these methods in order to benefit humankind. When Usui recovered from his near fatal illness, he began to discuss his experiences with his family and family priest. They were outraged at his claims of seeing enlightened deities and the Tendai priest beat him over the head and chased him out of the Temple. How could a man of his learning experience such profound realisations?

Determined to find the answers to his questions about this vision, Usui eventually met a Shingon Bonze, Watanabe, who recognised Usui's tremendous spiritual potential and took him on as a student. Usui then studied Shingon Buddhism, as well as many other religions to find a broader understanding of the healing traditions.

Mikao Usui spent much time and money pursuing his new-found spiritual path by studying and collecting Buddhist scriptures. In particular, he studied Buddhist healing techniques and invested an enormous amount of money collecting old medical texts. Usui had good political and academic connections and had many contacts in various countries searching for texts. For example, in Bombay, India, merchants travelling along the silk route through

Tibet to China were given gold to find secret Buddhist healing texts. Usui was particularly interested in obtaining texts from Tibet.

Kyoto was home to many large and extensive Buddhist libraries and monasteries that had collections of ancient texts. Usui did much of his research there. For many years, Usui continued to collect, study and practice these medical texts. He became an advanced practitioner and master of meditation.

Over time, Usui became a respected and learned Buddhist teacher with a following of devoted students. They met regularly and Usui would teach from the texts that he had been collecting. The focus of his teachings was on healing and benefiting humankind through healing practice. They practiced elaborate rituals for averting newly created diseases that were ravaging Japan, as well as esoteric practices for healing every type of illness.

Mikao Usui was truly a man ahead of his time. He went against the social norms of his day, which were very sectarian and class oriented. Usui believed that everyone should have access to healing methods, regardless of their religious beliefs. He wanted to find a way to offer these powerful methods to the common person and to find a way and method to achieve this end. Out of his great determination, he vowed that he would some day find a way to develop a healing system that would cure every type of disease and could be taught to anyone, regardless of class, background, or religious beliefs.

It was during the late 1890s that Usui came in contact with a series of manuscripts that held the keys he had sought for so many years. Armed with his new-found knowledge he decided to do a retreat to perhaps gain a deeper understanding of the methods he had discovered.

Dr Usui decided his meditation retreat would be at Mt Kurama. It is not known how long he spent in meditation, some accounts suggest it was 21 days. At the completion of his time on Kurama he gained an understanding of these methods and realised the way to heal as a complete system. After much contemplation and careful consideration he decided to share these teachings with others. Through the distillation of years of study and practice, Usui was able to perceive a method for bringing the essence of these Buddhist practices to the masses. Usui called this healing method 'Reiki'.

Usui first practiced his newly discovered method on his family and friends. Then he began to offer his healing method to the lower class district of Kyoto. Kyoto is a religious centre and the people in the streets are taken in and cared for with each family looking out for its own. Usui opened his home to many and for seven years he brought Reiki to them. This gave him the opportunity to perfect and refine his new healing method. Meanwhile, he continued to hold regular classes for his growing 'circle' of Buddhist followers, and further developed and refined his system.

In 1921, Usui moved to Tokyo where he worked as the secretary to Pei Gotoushin, the Prime Minister of Tokyo. He opened a Reiki clinic in Harajuku, outside Tokyo and began to set up classes and teach his system of Reiki. Some of his foremost students, who received the teachings, include:

- Taketomi, who was a naval officer;
- Wanami;
- Five Buddhist nuns; and
- Kozo Ogawa. Ogawa opened a Reiki clinic in Shizuoka City. He was very active in the administration of the Reiki society (Reiki Gakkai). He passed on his work to his relative, Fumio Ogawa, who is still alive today.

In 1922, Usui reportedly founded the Reiki society, called Usui Reiki Ryoho Gakkai, and acted as its first president. This society was open to those who had studied Usui's Reiki. This society still exists today and there have been six presidents since Usui:

Mr Jusaburo Ushida 1865-1935,
Mr Kanichi Taketomi 1878-1960,
Mr Yoshiharu Watanabe (unknown - 1960),
Mr Hoichi Wanami 1883-1975,
Ms Kimiko Koyama 1906-1999,
and the current president Mr Masayoshi Kondo.

On September 1, 1923 the devastating Kanto earthquake struck Tokyo and its surrounding areas. Most of the central part of Tokyo was leveled and totally destroyed by fire. Over 140,000 people were killed. In one instance, 40,000 people were incinerated to death when a fire tornado swept across the open area where they had sought safety. These fires were started when the quake hit at midday, when countless hibachi charcoal grills were ready to cook lunch. The wood houses quickly ignited as they collapsed from the tremors. Three million homes were destroyed leaving countless homeless. Over 50,000 people suffered serious injuries. The public water and sewage systems were destroyed and it took years for rebuilding to take place.

In response to this catastrophe, Usui and his students offered Reiki to countless victims. His clinic soon became too small to handle the throng of patients, so in February 1924, he built a new clinic in Nakano, outside Tokyo. His fame spread quickly all over Japan and he began receiving invitations from all over the country to come and teach his healing methods. Usui was awarded a Kun San To from the Emperor, which is a very high award (much like an honorary doctorate), given to those who have done honourable work. His fame soon spread throughout the region and many prominent healers and physicians began requesting teachings from him.

Just prior to this devastating earthquake in 1923, Usui had

begun teaching a simplified form of Reiki to the public in order to meet increasing demand. Two of his most notable students included:

- Toshihiro Eguchi, who studied with Usui in 1923. Eguchi was the most prominent of his students who reportedly taught thousands of students before the war. It is largely through Eguchi that Reiki has continued on in Japan; and
- Chujiro Hayashi, who studied with Usui from 1922. Hayashi was one of the first of Usui's non-Buddhist students. Hayashi used the knowledge learned from Usui to open a clinic in Tokyo. He replaced some of the format of Usui's teachings and created a system of 'degrees'. He also developed a more complex set of hand positions suitable for clinic use. Hayashi's clinic employed a method of healing that required several practitioners to work on one client at the same time to maximise the energy flow. One way Hayashi encouraged practitioners to his clinic was to give Level first empowerments in return for a three month commitment as unpaid help. After this time he would offer the better students the second Level in return for a further nine month commitment. Those who completed this had the chance of receiving the teacher's level or third degree. After two years' further commitment (which involved assisting Hayashi in the classroom), practitioners were taught the empowerments and

were allowed to teach. Hayashi subsequently passed his knowledge to Mrs Takata, who was responsible for bringing Reiki to America in the 1970s. It should be stressed that the actual content of the Reiki system known in the West today bears but a fragment of Usui's original Reiki system. Usui taught a simplified form of Reiki to Hayashi and in turn, Hayashi introduced new elements and structures to the Reiki system. Further to this, Mrs Takata changed and added new material again to the system. So when Reiki finally came to the West, the Usui system had changed quite significantly and bore little resemblance to its former roots.

Usui quickly became very busy as requests for teachings of Reiki continued to grow. He travelled throughout Japan (not an easy undertaking in those days), to teach and give Reiki empowerments. This started to take its toll on his health and he began experiencing mini-strokes from stress. Usui then left for a teaching tour in the western part of Japan. Finally, on March 9, 1926, while in Fukuyama, Usui died of a fatal stroke. He was 62 years old.

Usui's body was cremated and his ashes were placed in a temple in Tokyo. Shortly after his death, students from the Reiki society in Tokyo erected a memorial stone at Saihoji Temple in the Toyatama district in Tokyo. According to the inscription on his memorial stone, Usui taught Reiki to over 2,000 people. Many of these students began their own clinics and founded Reiki schools and societies. By the 1940s there were about 40 Reiki schools spread all over Japan. Most of these schools taught the simplified method of Reiki that Usui had developed. Another more secret Reiki Society (the Reiki Gakkai) continued to maintain the esoteric tradition.

Since this time Reiki has flourished in the West and much of the Reiki that ones finds in Japan today is actually imported from western teachers.

In 1999, some of the original methods as taught by the Reiki Gakkai were revealed for the first time in Vancouver, Canada. These practices were taught by Mr Doi, a member of the Reiki Gakkai and many teachers now use these original methods, dating their origin back to Mikao Usui.

Bibliography

Reference material;

Prana the secret of Yogic Healing by Atreya

Power Yoga by Beryl Bender Birch

The Tao of Reiki by Lawrence Ellyard

Eastern Body, Western Mind by Anodea Judith

Elena Tchernychko at Kirlean Research Ltd for the Gas Discharge Visualisation Images.

Video publications by John De Ruiter, Oasis, Edmonton, Canada

Recommended Reading

Anything by: Ken Carey

Unveiling Reality by John De Ruiter

Empower Your Life With Reiki by Richard Ellis

The Tao of Reiki by Lawrence Ellyard

Any chakra books by Anodea Judith

Anything by: Tom Robbins

Contact

Contact the author Richard Ellis at www.practicalreiki.com
or through the publishers at Random House

霊
気